# A MAN POSSESSED

The Case History
of Sigmund Freud

# A MAN POSSESSED

# The Case History of Sigmund Freud

*by*
*Nat Morris*

**REGENT HOUSE**
Los Angeles

Library of Congress
Catalog Card Number 73-92383
ISBN 0-911238-53-0
Manufactured in the United States of America

# CONTENTS

# Preface

For a layman to challenge Freud's authority may seem presumptious but I do have one highly valid credential — experience. Experience, thorough and complete, was my Yale College and my Harvard. It ran the gamut from trusting belief, through actual trials on the couch, only to end with the conviction that psychoanalysis was the creation of a perverse egomaniac. My first chapter delineates that experience.

Today the layman is not at too great a disadvantage in technical matters for eventually every scientific advance is explained in lay terms. In its first stages, however, only qualified authorities may understand it. Darwin's theory was recognized at first only by his scientific peers; today it is taught in our public schools.

But typical of Freud's perversity, he reversed the procedure for his professional contemporaries immediately and coldly rejected his theories. He then appealed to the public as a victim of narrow, unscientific prejudices. Through his phenomenal glibness, his enormous literary production, inexhaustible energy and hypnotic powers, he attracted believers in his narcissistic image as a martyr to truth. Psychoanalysis then became a popular movement fed by Freud's promises of superior insight for believers.

By addressing himself to laymen, Freud not only foiled his professional opponents but won fame and fortune. He also created a very lucrative and easy profession — the paid listener. Now the public is constantly bombarded with psychological advertising in books, lectures, periodicals and other media, advising and exhorting us to "know" ourselves, but also hinting that this self understanding can be facilitated through professional consultations.

My suggestions to my fellow laymen stresses another note: Know something about the men who have chosen so indolent a profession as psychoanalysis, their technique for inducing belief in Freud's delusions and luring people to the couch for interminable courses at such exorbitant fees.

Novels and biographies proffered as psychological case histories are commonplace; the educational world has gone on a psychological binge. Only the other day, the University of California at Los Angeles announced a series of lectures, "Psychiatry for Non-Psychiatrists."

In 1955 I got into the act with *The Case History of Sigmund Freud* which identified him as the standard, the one and only case recognized in psychoanalysis, complete with a lust for mother incest, parricidal hates, castration terror, and anal eroticism but above all, narcissism (egomania). Every incumbent of the couch, and many who have not lain there, are made to fit that one, standardized case. They may as well name everybody Sigmund and start a new calendar with May 6, 1856.

After publishing Freud's case history, I was always haunted by the notion that a vital clue to his frenetic strivings was still lacking; a clue which would clinch my case beyond all doubt. Then, in continuing to read the never ending stream of Freudiana gushing from adulants, that vital clue at last turned up. To my intense satisfaction, the discoverer was a layman like myself, Irving Stone. Blissfully ignorant of the significance of his find, Stone exposes the incredibly grotesque circumstances in Freud's "primal scene."

Upon this and other traumatic events in Freud's tortured life I have formulated my diagnosis of him as a man possessed; a man convulsed with a frantic urge to achieve a glittering success to refute his father's taunt that he would "never amount to anything."

Jung, favored by the closest intimacy with Freud while not entirely dazzled by him, divined that he was "possessed by a daemon, vouchsafed an overwhelming revelation." Jung identified that revelation as Freud's *numinosum,* something "inexpressible, terrifying and directly experienced," but did not venture to probe into the nature of Freud's revelation.

My version is that it was no more than his conceit that he possessed the divine right of genius and no matter how perverse and outrageous his utterances and actions were, he could do no wrong and he must never admit being wrong.

Though fatal to his scientific credibility, that attitude was conducive of success. Could any salesman succeed at selling unless he was fanatically convinced his product was saleable despite all evidence it was a gyp? For no matter how insipid were Freud's formulation, they were couched by a master of prose, by a man inherently shrewd, resourceful and ruthless, endowed with phenomenal energy and persistence. How he promoted the psychoanalytic movement and violated every principle of scientific and medical principles is the theme of this work.

Nat Morris

Los Angeles, California

## CHAPTER 1

# An Independent Judgment

*"The teachings of psychoanalysis are based upon an incalculable number of observations and experience, and no one who has not repeated these observations upon himself or upon others is in a position to arrive at an independent judgment."*

This defiant manifesto is typical Freud. The "incalculable number of observations" he boasted were merely his own introspections, for his own case occupied him throughout his long, tormented life. The "teachings of psychoanalysis" were simply the results of his self observation, which he transmuted into universal attributes of human nature. He was the perfect example of the Oedipus complex, as a careful scrutiny of his case will disclose.

Those who have writhed upon his couch for futile hour after futile hour, attempting to "repeat these observations upon himself" as I have, only to find they are not only inapplicable but only prolong their misery at unnecessary time and expense, are certainly in "a position to arrive at an independent judgment." The joker is that only after escaping from the psychic spell Freud could induce, is an independent judgment possible. When Adler, Rank, Ferenczi and Jung among others attempted to render such judgments, the consequences are only too well known.

As analyses go, my Freudian encounter was comparatively brief, about one-hundred and fifty hours on three
different couches. Thousands of hours logged over ten
years or more, are fairly common now. Hours logged, however, is not the only criterion; the period of belief in Freud's
dubious propositions must also be considered. Mine persisted for about twelve years, from the age of eighteen
to thirty.

Those years and several prior to them, were burdened
with a well recognized symptomatology, including personality transformation, loss of memory, lack of concentration, etc., etc. At the same time, a counteractive feeling
also persisted that the change from a confident, aggressive
personality to an uncertain, hesitant one was only temporary and could be removed through competent psychological services.

Why not? My health has been almost perfect throughout my life, now in its seventh decade. Abnormal cravings
or vices have never bothered me. It seemed foolish not
to secure professional advice. Since psychoanalysis was
the most widely discussed and advertised method, I
believed and sought the couch for relief. In the process,
my frustrations and torments were intensified. My recovery began the instant I cast off belief in Freud. It happened
in this way during the thirties in New York one evening
between seances:

Somewhat depressed, I had stopped at a bar for a drink.
Seated near me was a homosexual who struck up a conversation. He was diffidently polite and spoke with very evident erudition so out of respect for his good manners and
intelligence, I did not brush him off. He was evidently
not just a fag on the make, but merely lonely.

As we talked, it soon became obvious to me that his
intellectual plane was not only far above mine but also
that of my analyst's. He spoke so interestingly about literature and kindred topics, that a sudden impulse led me
to steer the conversation to psychoanalysis. And then,
as if it were another person speaking, I heard myself admit
for the first time to anyone that my analysis was then

going on, but that "It's about over now."

"I would never have guessed it. You don't look like the neurotic type," was his surprised reply. He then confessed that he had once tried analysis himself, only to run out of money, mentioning it as if it were of little importance, without conveying disappointment nor any wish to try again. This was quite a contrast to my own desperation in seeking analysis, as if my very life depended on it.

As is characteristic of a state of restricted consciousness, my thoughts and feelings during those days were fleeting and subliminal. Now I recognize that as my chief symptom but it was never brought to my attention in psychoanalysis.

After finishing my drink, we parted but our conversation had had a powerful effect and left me eager and impatient for the next seance several days later. Once on the couch, I immediately expressed a wish to "quit."

"You can quit if you want to," came the Voice from behind.

For the last time, I dismounted from the couch and after a perfunctory good-bye, quickly left, as if afraid he would rescind his unexpected permission to "quit." The business of termination had taken no more than five minutes but there was no doubt in my mind that it was a termination, once and for all.

On reaching the street, I began to walk on air. A highly pleasant state of relief pervaded my entire system, right down to my shoe laces. Every nerve was relaxed; all tension gone, and for about a week, this pleasant euphoria persisted. Life had become enjoyable; a capacity for pleasure was awakened.

As the euphoria subsided, I began to wonder. Certainly my exhilaration could not be attributed to a successful analysis, but merely to the fact that it was over. In wondering why, my memory started working and it was if I was awakening from a long sleep. I recalled that in parting the analyst seemed reluctant to shake hands, was quite indifferent to my very evident relief and offered neither advice, encouragement nor good wishes. He was just as anxious for me to go as I to leave.

Reflecting upon this brought an onrush of recall; a veil of amnesia lifted as I remembered sarcasm after sarcasm, slightly veiled insults; a complete indifference for my welfare; never one word of encouragement. This was particularly galling in view of the remarkable lift my chance acquaintance, a deviant at that, had given me with a few words.

The lift was the result of a beneficial suggestion but the same power of suggestion had lured me into the Freudian trap; suggestion in the form of auto-suggestion was responsible for my so-called neurosis as I will disclose, and was the dominating influence in the analysis. For example, it had seemed perfectly natural in that last seance not to expect any advice or summary of my case because in the very first seance, just as I was about to start "free associating," he had warned (suggested) that he could "guarantee nothing." He had interpolated this warning as if he had suddenly realized it must be put on record. Having absolved himself of any obligation to guarantee anything, he made no effort to do anything.

Eventually his indifference developed into a hostility known as "counter-transference" in the jargon for reasons I will recount. This analyst incidentally was fully accredited, having studied in Vienna and undoubtedly heard the Master himself. He had been referred to me by Paul Schilder and is still in practice. Though never prominent in psychoanalysis he once made the newspaper headlines when the Supreme Court nullified the refusal of the State Department to issue him a passport on the grounds he was a Communist. His vindictiveness toward me, typical of dissidents, among other reasons may have been due to my lukewarm faith in Freud and also because he sensed I was not Communist material.

My two previous attempts at analysis had been abortive and left me determined not to try again unless there were indications of improved techniques and quicker results. Brief as my attempts were, at bottom I felt my case was comparatively simple and should have been easily relieved. Occasionally I checked the journals for new developments when one day I ran across Schilder's article[1] advocating active methods and shorter treatments. That was it; no more boring, desultory free associations but a quick and definite solution, once and for all.

Upon seeing Schilder, he referred me to my third analyst as his fees were beyond my reach. Nevertheless he charged me his fee, ten dollars for his time and the referral. Making the arrangements for what I believed would be a new approach with a better technique, some fifteen months later this fiasco terminated as described. However, I do believe that in a way it was successful for it dissolved belief in psychoanalysis and restored a capacity to reflect, remember and judge. With this, came "abreaction," which is the indication of a successful treatment. True, it was a violent abreaction but the benefits were real and measurable.

A few incidents will illustrate the possible reasons for the man's hostility (counter-transference): One day I impulsively remarked that sometimes "psychoanalysis seems like a lot of bull shit." To prove it was not "bull shit" (repeating my profanity) he said that even dogs were homosexual. For a fleeting moment, his proof appeared ridiculous, but it was only for a fleeting moment, quickly lost in amnesia.

This introduced homosexuality into the analysis. Gradually and subliminally I began to accept some homosexual involvement although in real life such has never been suggested to me. Later it dawned upon me that this accounted for my willingness to talk to the homosexual I met and when he made no advances it was because he sensed there was nothing homosexual in my make-up, which was gratifying.

One day I asked the analyst some quite personal questions.

"What kind of a life would I lead," he whimpered, "if I had to answer all my patients' questions?"

Yet he had once evinced some surprise because I never

mentioned such intimacies as where I went, what I ate, etc. This sounded rather asinine to me; I was in his office for a far reaching purpose, not to gossip, but if intimacy was expected, a beautiful opportunity soon arose. One day a pretty blonde, matching his gigoloish good looks was quickly admitted while I waited at his request in the ante-room. She stayed only a few minutes but in avoiding my glance, she aroused a resentment carried to the couch.

After verifying she was his wife, a sudden impulse to say something spiteful seized me. With the license encourages as "free associations" out popped that she was beautiful and that "I would not mind laying her."

He said nothing, but the man possessed a fearful means of vengeance. I am quite sure that his hostility commenced about that time, although there was also some wrangling about my responsibility for Schilder's fee which I delayed paying until he commanded me to do so, and also for what he said was my insulting way of tossing his fee upon his desk.

A psychoanalyst operates much like a spy or secret agent. There is something inherently treacherous and stealthy about their sitting out of sight. This fellow knew of my dissatisfaction with my other two attempts and my fear of sinking again into the same morass and that is what eventually happened. The process of abreaction left me with a burning desire for a face to face confrontation to complete my transactions in full.

Shortly before quitting, I had seen a young, attractive patient whom I had seen only once before, when beginning. It was a shock; here was a young girl who appeared whole-some and intelligent, mired in the Freudian quicksand. In my anger, I remembered her and left a note with the elevator man asking her to phone me.

She never did, nor did the analyst respond to my calls and letters. One night I confronted him as his door opened between patients and demanded an explanation.

"I can refuse to answer a letter if I want to," he said childishly, then added abjectively:

"You can do anything you want to to me, but leave

my patients out of it." This admitted both his malice and that the girl had blabbed. When I accused him of being a petty, spiteful quack only aggravating my troubles, his malicious, sadistic grin was chilling to see. It was a half-mad, gloating look, as if he revelled in his revenge. That one, startling look at the almost insane expression on his face went far toward restoring my mental equilibrium, for even in my wildest moments could I ever bring myself to double-crossing someone who had placed their confidence in me. Yet this man showed no compunction whatsoever for the fact that he had accepted fees for his malicious, frustrating tactics.

When I went to see Schilder, his face was a polite, bland mask. He was probably thoroughly familiar with the aimless course of Freudian analysis for that had prompted his paper, which would naturally be regarded as heresy and an attempt to form an independent movement. It was also quite possible that he had referred me to his young colleague to enlist his affiliation.

Though he listened politely, Schilder acknowledged no responsibility for the conduct of his protegee. Actually Schilder was a remote, detached individual as the manner of his death would indicate. One date he attempted to cross Times Square while deeply immersed in a book and heedless of the traffic. He was killed by an automobile.

The second analyst of my experiences worked in the same building as Schilder's protegee. Some five years before he had been recommended to me by Sandor Lorand, his teacher. This transaction had lasted only about twenty seances because my employer, a ruthless corporation, kept demanding more and more overtime which interfered with appointments. This analyst, a sly, insignificant little fellow, probably suspecting both my unsuitability for analysis and my aversion for him, quickly suggested calling things off until a more suitable time.

The analysis had been contracted for at three visits per week, but after paying my first bill, he suddenly demanded five visits per week. When asked why, he merely said that's the way it must be. In my eagerness

to complete analysis, under the illusion it was a scientifi-
cally authentic method and my aversion for the man would
disappear, I weakly consented, believing that five visits
per week would complete it sooner. As I eventually
learned, everything in psychoanalysis is completely contrary to reason and five times per week would require
more weeks than three visits per week.

Later I also discovered another reason for his demand
besides increasing his income. Evidently he had gleaned
from my disclosures that my salary would support two
more visits. Since Freud recommended carrying on analyses in a state of "abstinence" which meant denying
pleasures to the patient, he complied. A patient with diver-
sions could also find analysis very boring, as it really
is, and wish to end it.

One day I impulsively asserted that Freud seemed
somewhat infantile. It was a sudden display of an alter
ego, a stronger, aggressive side.

"Everybody is infantile," he said hastily and the idea
was instantly dropped.

On another occasion, he interpreted a dream as my
attempt to reduce him to my level. Between seances, the
recollection of this insulting remark rankled. In the next
seance I reminded him about it and told him he would
not have to descend very far to get down to my level.
With characteristic evasiveness, he said nothing.

When I phoned this fellow some five years later, he
remembered me well and evidently thought I wished to
change analysts. Possibly he had seen me in the building
for the first thing he asked was: "Are you in analysis
now?"

When I told him that my mission was to discover what
the analysis had been all about, not sensing that I really
was there to demand an accounting for his shoddy tactics,
he answered in a mechanical, sing song voice, much like
a street hawker:

"We analyze a few dreams, a few errors, slips of the
tongue and so on," he droned, intimating it was a sort
of game, nothing serious mind you; no hard feel-

ings. . . .

It was ghastly; he seemed to have no therapeutic motivation whatsoever nor any idea of the discomfort and pain in neuroses. Yet this cold fish had once had access to my innermost thoughts despite my strong aversion for him. When I told him that his notion of analysis was not worth the time and money it cost me, he jerked off his chair, shouting with deep emotion:

"What it cost you? What do you think it cost me?"

It was laughable. He was just another victim of the Pied Piper of Vienna, as badly hoodwinked as his patients. Once discovering the fraud, he continued sitting behind a couch to recoup his investment. Freud had found himself in the same quandary after he was forced to admit he had swallowed the seduction phantasies of his female patients but he confessed that he continued because he did not know what else to do.

Wondering how I had fallen for Freud's propaganda led to re-reading his *General Introduction to Psychoanalysis*.[2] In the light of actual experience it was immensely rewarding for providing an insight into the subtle influences of suggestion. To my astonishment, the glib introduction by G. Stanley Hall, testifying to "thousands of cures" had had the strongest affect in inducing my belief in Freud. It was this testimonial, purportedly from an impartial outsider, that had kept me persisting in analysis, continually suppressing my own fleeting doubts and misapprehensions.

How could I have known, at the age of eighteen when reading this ballyhoo of G. Stanley Hall that he had no proof whatsoever of "thousands of cures," for he had never practiced psychoanalysis. At the time he wrote his testimonial, it was doubtful whether "thousands" had ever yet been on the couch. Hall had been instrumental in inviting Freud to Clark University thereby paving the way for his eventual dominance here. His foreword had been arranged by Freud's nephew, Edward L. Bernays, who confesses in his autobiography[3] that he knew nothing of psychoanalysis, but undertook its promotion for the glory of the family. He proved his uncle's couch could be propagandized as easily as the breakfast cereals, automobiles, musical comedies, ballet careers or other commodities or interests of his clients.

Despite Hall's ballyhoo about cures, Freud did not present even one successful therapy in his book. He discussed only four or five cases but all were either incomplete or failures. Nor in his entire writings, has he ever presented one complete and genuine case of a successful treatment with psychoanalysis, performed through his techniques of free association, analyzing dreams, dissolving transferences, etc., etc. Actually he was not only pessimistic about the therapeutic value of his system but at the apex of his fame discouraged all attempts to shorten treatment or concentrate upon therapeutic results. Attempts to concentrate upon healing rather than the validity of his observations aroused his awesome capacity for invective, as loosed upon Adler and Stekel and even upon Ferenczi, one of his most loyal and adulant disciples.

As a propagandist, Freud was without peer. His nephew Bernays, amasser of millions as a paid publicist, is a mere amateur in comparison to his uncle Sigmund. All his writings were but one long commercial, advertising himself as a martyr to truth. His achievement in disguising both his morbid, cantankerous personality and his frustrating, exorbitantly priced method is a masterpiece of misrepresentation.

Freud's *General Introduction to Psychoanalysis* was a powerful instrument of conversion by presenting "some of the incalculable number of observations" upon which he based his system. His technique for convincing the susceptible which proved so effective is readily discernible in the first lecture. This was devoted to blocking off prior impressions and beliefs by warning that his ideology was new and epochal, exploring hitherto undiscovered territory and was unrelated to any other system of thought.

It is masterly self promotion. Freud subtly represented himself as a fighter for truth, battling against ignorant but powerful prejudices. He played for sympathy and pleaded exemption from conforming to the requirement to supply verifiable data to prove his contentions. Through his remarkable glibness, he created an image of intrepid integrity and intellectual supremacy.

It is the technique of the big lie all over again. Actually Freud could not adapt his thinking and behavior to established rules and precedents. Nor could he understand others except in relation to himself. His aversion for other systems of thought was born of his jealousy and inability to appreciate competing ideas. Reading the plethora of his writings will confirm this for references to other schools and thinkers in psychology are practically non-existent.

Consequently it is readily apparent why he was driven to create his own system, independent of all others because then he could deny the validity of criticisms which were unjustifiable unless his "incalculable observations" were repeated. Critics versed in scientific methods decried psychoanalysis because it was not verifiable by methods familiar to them. Freud merely hurled their accusations of scientific incompetence back at them but the clever facility of his language obscured his chicanery.

Still, Freud did have his moments of honest candor. In his autobiography[4] he admitted having no gift for the natural sciences. He also admitted that after forty-one years of medical activity, he had never been a physician in the "proper sense." Yet psychoanalysis has been accepted both as a science and a nostrum.

These facts were of course unknown to lay readers like myself delving into *A General Introduction to Psychoanalysis*. The chapters on errors, slips of the tongue and other every day psychopathology were plausible enough to my eighteen year old mind, fascinated by Freud's provocative, readable style. But when he delved into dreams, after only a few paragraphs I literally flung the book against the wall. This was gypsy stuff for sure. For several weeks I had had enough of Freud. There was something fishy about him; he was getting difficult to swallow.

In recalling this initial repugnance for this dreamology, I rued the contrite mood that lured me to reconsider and read again, thereby succumbing to his warning in the very first lecture against holding to prior concepts and beliefs.

Of Freud himself, after a sympathetic reaction to him as a fellow Jew, doubts continued to arise because of this very sympathy which could cloud "independent judgment." Moreover, his pleading for special consideration, smacked of the "chosen people" theme, offensive both to Christians and enlightened Jews.

Many of his autobiographical disclosures aroused further aversion. His confession of being scolded by a maid who had seen him spit on the outside stairs when arriving to make a house call, was a discredit to a physician. His cold reaction to his father's account of how his hat was tossed into the street by an anti-Semite, was also repelling. His shocking confession of urinating in his parent's bedroom, conveyed something pathological in his make-up, though I never dreamt of its real significance.

Freud also asserted he would instantly command ladies "dressed in all their finery" to go back to close the door to his office if they had left it open behind them. This oversight betrayed they believed there was little danger of others arriving to his modestly furnished office for it only happened when the waiting room was empty. This impressed me with Freud's uncanny mind reading ability.

On the other hand, Freud betrayed his own glaring frailties in his tale about a woman neighbor who had called to borrow some reading matter. In a rhapsody of enthusiasm, he recommended *She* by Sir H. Rider Haggard. After accepting his recommendation, the woman spitefully asked if it contained such intimate self exposures as were in his writings. Deeply hurt, Freud bleated childishly about the sacrifice of his privacy in the interests of scientific progress, only to reap such unappreciation. It was this incident which prompted me to blurt out in one seance that Freud was "infantile." How infantile he really was, astounds the imagination.

Though his material on errors and so on, was interesting reading, it seemed of little significance therapeutically, but the account of his good results during his apprenticeship to Breuer were very convincing and impressive, as they actually were. He induced recall of traumatic incidents directly and effectively, leading to abreaction and relief.

That inspired my hope psychoanalysis would be my salvation by uncovering a long forgotten traumatic event at the root of my troubles. That hope had kept me persevering despite all the discouraging incidents I have related.

It was only logical for me to believe Freud had improved upon his earlier methods by eliminating hypnotism. Who would suspect that in his egomania he had perverted hypnotism ot compel belief in his ideology while at the same time depreciating its therapeutic value?

Eventually it struck me with a sickening impact that my subjection to the couch was a typical manifestation of hypnotism. My pleasant euphoria and the subsequent lifting of amnesia was simply awakening from a long standing trance. The hypnotist wakes his subject by telling him to open his eyes whereupon he will feel greatly refreshed, better than he has ever felt before. The hypnotist can restore memory for everything during the trance, or obliterate that memory if he so chooses.

The salient characteristic of the hypnotized is their suggestibility. But hypnotism can also be unwittingly self induced, bringing on a prolonged state of trance, with short awakenings and relapses which give the impression of an erratic, unstable personality. The hypnotized are subject to bizarre ideas, delusions and aberrant impulses. They are divided personalities, indecisive, unable to resolve conflicting impulses, try though they may. However, innate character acts as check against suggestions foreign to one's nature, as hypnotists acknowledge. In my own case, psychoanalysis was only partially accepted. The analysts rarely attempted any orthodox interpretations, sensing my skepticism.

In his remarkable study, *New Concepts of Hypnosis,*[5]

Bernard C. Gindes reports a remarkable example of how
hypnotist can be rejected by a subject in a deep trance.
A physician who dabbled in hypnotism succeeded in hypnotizing his wife but when he tried to question her, she
went into an alarming state of catalepsy. Unable to restore
her, he called in Dr. Gindes who did. Later the woman
told him that her husband was deeply jealous of her pre-
marital love life and she suspected he would pry into it
during her trance. In self defense, she went mute lest
she betray her innermost secrets.

Some such state of paralysis of the will had long
plagued me. Unfortunately one becomes inarticulate in
that state of mind, unable to express the vague, shadowy
thoughts and impulses flitting across the stream of consciousness. This also makes a joke of the Freudian procedure for relying upon the patient for disclosures without
the help, cooperation and encouragement a physician
should exercise, is futile. However, futility and frustration are very profitable for the psychoanalyst, as will
be disclosed.

The amnesia which develops on the couch, led me to
forget what brought me there — the hope that recovering
some buried event of the past was the curative goal. That
hunch proved sound for that is exactly what happened,
though it only came after renouncing psychoanalysis. It
was baffling to realize that not once during my twelve
years of inward scanning, the elusive memory never
emerged on or off the couch or in a dream. That dreams
are the "royal road to the unconscious" proved to be
another of Freud's myths. Another myth is that an
untreated neurosis would last "ten years for every one
of treatment."[6] In my case, the all revealing insight
arrived dramatically only a few months after terminating
psychoanalysis, in this way:

One Sunday I strolled to Central Park to watch
baseball. Some excellent teams played there in those days,
usually later in the afternoon. One game was about to
start but there was some hitch. A man evidently managing
one of the teams was approaching spectator after spectator

with some request, only to be refused.

Finally I heard him say very courteously that a catcher was needed for whom the necessary gear was available. A state of acute anxiety then assailed me, accompanied by conflicting emotions, fearing both that he would ask me to catch and that he would not. If he did, there could be no refusal, but neither could I admit being an experienced catcher.

But ask me he did. In a few moments, equipped with a mask, chest protector and mitt, trying to hide my nervousness, my catching chore began. With the protective gear my anxiety gradually subsided for all the players were hopeless dubs, and my own clumsiness from lack of practice was not noticed. After only a few innings, the game ended for the players did not seem overly interested. Baseball may have been prescribed for them as a form of therapy, for they were an odd looking crew.

In pondering that brief catching experience, it gradually dawned upon me that the double reaction of both fearing being asked to catch, and not being asked accompanied by nervous anxiety was a significant symptom. Catching again behind the plate, exposed to the danger of foul tips but with protective gear, had somehow worked a highly beneficial effect. Protected by a mask, when the batter swung at a pitch, I did not flinch but caught the ball if he missed.

In my boyhood, baseball was a passion; we played almost all day long. But what was a great pleasure one day turned to misery when the onerous job of catching was foisted upon me. Without a mask or chest protector, the exposure to foul tips ricocheting off a bat was terrifying. It was my introduction to fear and panic but admitting fear was humiliating. Consequently, for inning after inning and game after game, my fear was repressed until some kind of self control was achieved, though only after a terrific inward struggle. A tendency to flinch at every swing of the bat made catching gruesome, but somehow I became locked into this impossible situation and could not escape.

To go into all the details would make a guinea pig of me. Besides, this type of emotional reaction is very well known and has been described innumerable times. Why this traumatic memory become suppressed; why it never emerged despite my eager attempts, is beyond me. In later years after becoming acquainted with endocrinology in selling medical books, it seemed to me that adrenalin rushing into the blood stream worked a demoralizing effect by causing my heart to pound at a fearful rate. A tremendous effort had to be made to endure the pain. By some superhuman effort it was done but only by an all out effort probably possible only once in a lifetime.

Conditioned to endure pain, my sufferance of the Freudian exploitation indicated some form of self hypnosis was present. Only through exploiting a hypnotic condition, either induced on the couch or already present, can the Freudians carry their courses to such inordinate lengths as five, ten and even fifteen years with several different Sigmunds, all blandly indifferent and ineffective. Psychoanalysis is merely another chapter in the history of hypnotism, created by Freud in his trances. Sometimes he emerged from them amazed at his own delusions, as he often confessed to Fliess.

Freud merely hypnotized himself into believing he had discarded hypnotism and re-labeled the trance, "transference." Just as he could not always induce hypnotism, neither could he always induce transference. After his procedure became so long and involved, whether or not transference was established became difficult to determine. Was the patient addicted to interminable analysis became he was "transferred" (in love with the analyst) or because he was narcissistic (in love with hearing himself chatter)?

Who can tell? Certainly, the Freudians cannot. Nor do they care for their continued prosperity demands keeping their couches rented out, hour after hour, to incumbents talking and talking and paying and paying.

Nevertheless, the transference is intriguing to ponder.

Awe and respect may or may not accompany it; it did not in my case although a form of trance was present, fixed by my traumatic experience. Certainly there was great amenability to suggestion as the electrifying result of a complete stranger's casual observation attests. In retrospect, it seems to me that his matter of fact confession that he had tried psychoanalysis and had no particular regrets or wish to return to it, allayed my own anxious belief it was a matter of life or death.

Another powerful suggestive effect was inadvertently worked by the last analyst who said I could quit if I "wanted to." In some way, this worked to restore some freedom of will although his assent may have been maliciously inspired. Knowing my disappointment in my previous attempts, he may have thought he was inflicting another fiasco, an inconclusive termination settling nothing.

My disinclination for transference was disastrous, right from my first experience in Chicago at twenty-one. The analyst was young, pleasant and interested, with none of the offensive attributes of his successors. By all rights a transference should have become easy to establish. After only a few weeks, he asked:

"Do you find yourself thinking about me, wondering what I do and what I am like?"

"No," I curtly answered his amateurish question. From then on, my eagerness subsided and my confidence in him dissipated. Restlessness and dissatisfaction arrived; the money for him interfered with my pleasures. One day on the way to his office I lost his fee in one of Al Capone's gambling dens.

By the time I reached his office, the enormity of my defalcation put me in a state of shock. The matter of his fee was evaded and this evasion continued for several more sessions. He was just as cowardly and did not ask for his fee, but abruptly called off the analysis.

Psychoanalysts are unable to handle crises of any kind. They do not wish to be involved in the patient's symptoms, merely to observe them. They are trained that way and this poor fellow was no exception. He was incapable of malice but also of any intelligent effort.

Twenty years later, the same impulse to confront my former analysts, prompted me to see him. In the intervening years I had picked up a fair amount of medical knowledge and was aware that he had left me in the lurch by abandoning me without explanation. This is a violation of medical ethics.

Seeing him again was a shock. Twenty years of psychoanalysis had left him prematurely gray in his early forties, with a somewhat sad and forlorn look. He was distinctly ill at ease and had tried to avoid seeing me but bowed to my insistence. Just as he had twenty years before, he evaded clarifying matters, seemed completely disinterested and anxious for me to leave. He apologized for the pressure of his duties at the "Institute" and tried to impart a sacred, holy tone to the word and an air of importance to himself that his woebegone appearance belied.

It was no use. In arising to leave, I suddenly remembered the small balance still owed him. His evasiveness may have been due to feeling he was under no obligation to be frank in view of my debt. In turn, my feeling was it would be intolerable to owe such a wreck.

On being offered the money, he tried to make a show of refusing but quickly yielded, saying:

"If it will relieve your sense of guilt, I'll take it."

It was ghastly. This was the extent of his therapeutic motivation. It convinced me that ignoring his transference overtures left him feeling spurned. He however was a fellow who could have made an excellent physician for he was courteous, friendly and interested at first. Once inveigled into the Freudian trap which left him pursuing a futile, unsatisfying trade from which he could not escape, he drifted along passively listening to the never ending drone of free associations.

At least, there was comfort in knowing that analysts are greater victims of the Pied Piper of Vienna than their patients. A patient merely patronizes a form of treatment; the analyst must surrender his whole life.

## CHAPTER 2

# At the Worst

*"Psychoanalysis seems to bring out the worst in people."*

The unconscious mind has no perception of time, Freud often said. But his observation applied to him, for he displayed little awareness of the passage of time; the past was as fresh in his memory as the present moment. He forgot the years when emotion carried him away. The learned professor expounding his theories was as confident of his infallibility as the brilliant *primus* of the Sperl Gymnasium reciting his lessons.

Once fixed, Freud's traits remained immutable. His personality had been cast in the fire of childhood trauma and the boy was indistinguishable from the man except for the inevitable signs of age. But even when old, he moved as nimbly and gracefully as a youth.

Of Freud's many remarkable qualities, his energy, diligence and endurance, retained almost to the last day of his life, were incredible. Throughout his career, he maintained a crushing schedule of many hourly seances, followed by more hours of writing far into the night. He wrote easily and effortlessly, always in longhand, with his pen gliding over the paper smoothly; few erasures or corrections marred his manuscripts. It was a form of automatic writing, requiring no more than putting down on paper the thoughts he had had while sitting in a trance behind his patients.

He worked even in his sleep. Once he confided to Fliess
that when tired and confounded by some problem of dream
interpretation, he looked forward to sleep and the dreams
which would provide the solution.

With his phenomenal energy, Freud could not only out
walk, but out talk, out think, out write and out work just
about anyone in his milieu with only one possible exception — Ernest Jones, another demon for work and activity.
Freud tolerated few challenges to his authority, and these
only temporarily. His supremacy had to be undisputed.
The "crapule" (his own term for his followers) surrounding
him were as a rule meek and subservient.

Those who questioned his opinions soon reaped his
scorn and contempt. His capacity for hatred was as boundless as his energy. The two who challenged his authority
most openly, Stekel and Adler, became the objects of his
most spiteful invectives.

When Adler died suddenly on a street in Aberdeen,
Freud wrote this vicious obituary to Arnold Zweig:[1]

"For a Jew-boy out of a Viennese suburb, a death in
Aberdeen is an unheard-of career in itself and a proof
how far he had got on. The world really rewarded him
richly    for    his    service    of    contradicting
psychoanalysis."

Jew-boy! Only the most arrantly anti-Semitic use this
term. Did Freud scorn his own race? His capacity for
hatred was so enormous and pathological, it is not impossible. As he often attributed his long, bitter struggle for
recognition to the handicap of his Jewishness, it is proba-
ble he could vent his rage upon his own people.

He composed *Moses and Monotheism*[2] near the end of
his tormented life, questioning Moses' Jewish origins by
suggesting an Egyptian descent was possible. Freud's
thoroughly superfluous opinion was bitterly condemned
by Jewish scholars as worthy of an anti-Semite, as Ernest
Jones acknowledged in his official biography. Though the
Nazis were executing Jews by the thousands at the time,
Freud did not permit that to deter him from publishing his
version of the "truth."

Imagine the cold blooded cruelty inherent in characterizing the death of "Jew-boy" Adler on the street of a foreign city while a refugee from a homeland that had become a Nazi jungle, as an "unheard of career in itself." This outburst could have expressed a sadistic wish that Adler should have died only after prolonged suffering, instead of suddenly and painlessly.

Yet this overt hatred was not regarded as reflection on Freud's character by his admirers and is duly recorded in Freudiana. This inability of admirers to detect the serious flaws in his character may be due to the fact that psychoanalysis brought out the worst in them, as it had in Freud.

Admirers were usually hypnotically oblivious to his deficiencies; they absolved him from the judgments rendered of ordinary mortals. His indubitably formidable hypnotic powers stemmed from his beautiful brown eyes which glowed with a burning intensity. Fanatics usually possess such eyes; eyes that can transfix, entrance and compel blind belief.

His speech also had the same effect. Friz Wittels[3] who alternated obeisance with skeptical distrust, observed that nothing compared to listening to the "magic of his speech." Through his words, both written and spoken, he achieved the susceptibility he labeled "transference" instead of rapport, to avoid any suspicion he used hypnosis. But he could no more discard hypnotism than tear out his own eyes.

Once Freud achieved rapport in his private sittings, he then insinuated the material which he delighted in recovering as confirmation; a trick Fliess accused him of perpetrating. His pronunciamento that only those who had "repeated his observations," had a right to an independent judgment, betrays his confidence in his power to secure confirmation through inducing belief.

But hypnotism was only one of Freud's many talents. He was also a gifted linguist and learned Latin, Greek, English, Hebrew, French and other languages with little if any formal instruction. With the same gusto, his greedy memory sucked in mythology, philology, neurology, history, anthropology and what have you. His mind photographed on an indestructible but sensitive film. It was both a tremendous gift and a terrible curse; he could never forget and the burden of his memories was predominantly unpleasant. His hatred obliterated any acknowledgment of benefits from his associations with Adler, Stekel, Breuer and others who had once lent him valuable assistance. He remembered only their fancied slights.

What fuel sparked this incredible dynamo, driving him to superhuman efforts and inciting his endless hatreds and manias? Was it unexpended sexual resources, a libido blocked by an aversion for physical contact? (Freud never dallied as a youth in gay Vienna. He married at thirty, an admitted virgin; at forty, he acknowledged impotence and *finis* to sex.)

If there is any truth in Freud's assertion that the sex drive can be sublimated and re-directed, it would appear true in his case. The sexual orgasm he may not have been able to achieve possibly exploded as hate and jealousy. A complete catalog of his hates is impossible; Adler was probably Number One on his hate list; Stekel probably Number Two. When Breuer vacillated about Freud's sexual dogma, first believing then recanting, he too made the list. Freud comments about Breuer in his letters to Fliess, written when he was still under a financial obligation to him, were so vituperative they could not be published.[4]

The United States was high in his scorn, despite the happy hunting grounds it became for his disciples and despite winning his first international recognition here. Freud became miffed when a digestive upset he suffered here while away from his wife's sexcellent cooking, only met indifferent comment.

He also hated Vienna and its University, the scene of so many of his frustrations. His title as "professor extraordinarius," a somewhat mediocre reward was achieved through a bit of sordid wire pulling, hinging on the gift of a painting.[5] He also hated music for which he had no ear. He had a monumental hatred for medicine and there are many indications he rued his sudden impulse at seventeen to become a physician.

Depressing emotions were continually manifest through Freud's long and dreary life. He was attracted to the unpleasant; how else could his eagerness to listen to the most boring intimacies be explicable? The polarity of his nervous system gravitated toward the morbid, the perverse, the frustrating, irritating, quarrelsome, contentious and unreasonable. His demands upon the world for belief, for honors, favors, rewards and unbounded admiration knew no limits.

Yet, at times Freud could be genial and friendly, but only when his fears or jealousies were not aroused. When his professional interests and ambitions were not involved, he could be as pleasant as the next fellow. He played cards for fifty years with friends not associated with psychoanalysis with no record of any serious quarrel or dispute during those many years.

Freud also had a flair for practical matters as the manner he advertised and commercialized the business of psychoanalysis attests. In practical affairs, he was not dogmatic and displayed abilities which would have made him quite successful financially. According to Ernest Jones, he had an excellent grasp of business, currency exchange and legal complications.

For that matter, Ernest Jones was an even more capable administrator and for some years was the master mind behind the movement. It was Jones who organized the surveillance committee of the Seven Rings, to ferret out signs of possible defection and disloyalty to the cause. Jones acted for a number of years as trouble shooter and organizer of psychoanalytical societies in the United States, England and Canada. He also refereed disputes, recruited and screened applicants for Freudian franchises, and purged heretics.

Freud was superb as a propagandist and capitalized very cleverly upon the opposition stemming from the faculty of the University of Vienna, by attributing it to unreasonable bias and prejudice. One of the more droll features of his career was ridiculing the opposition of highly placed, eminent scholars and physicians as unreasonable, while at the same time contending that the delusions of the insane were logical. He promoted psychoanalysis both by accusing the University of bias against a new science and capitalizing upon the prestige of the institution by conniving to accelerate his appointment as *professor extraordinarius*.

At that stage of the movement in 1906, a whale swam into Freud's net. Eager for knowledge, fascinated by Freud's writings on dreams through his own predilection for the occult, Carl Jung called upon him in Vienna. Freud instantly recognized the tall, handsome Swiss psychiatrist as a invaluable recruit. They had much in common; each was somewhat of a rebel; both were fascinated by the symbolic, were avid readers and highly articulate.

The Jung association is one of the very few bright and pleasant chapters in Freud's frenetic life. Though it inevitably foundered on the reefs of Freud's insatiable ambition and dogmatism, years later he admitted sadly that Jung's departure was a "great loss."[6] Of no other dissident did he ever make such an admission.

Jung was a highly competent physician; his integrity was unquestionable. He was also talented in the arts and sculptured in stone as a hobby. Jung, however, differed from Freud in his autobiographical frankness.

Reading his *Memories, Dreams, Reflections*[7] is like peering into a glass enclosed brain. Jung was free of vindictive tendencies for when Freud and his cohorts attacked him viciously he never responded in kind, but merely attributed their ill nature to "short sightedness." Regardless of their differences, Jung retained his respect and acknowledged his debt to Freud throughout his life. It would have been impossible for Jung to gloat upon Freud's death as Freud had upon Adler's.

Their differing temperaments can be contrasted by the manner each decided upon medicine. Freud was suddenly inspired to become a physician by hearing a lecture on

Goethe's essay on nature. He had not entertained the notion before and his father was appalled, reminding him of his fear of blood. It was to no avail; Freud enrolled as a medical student possibly to spite his own father. For thirteen years, he remained at the University, often taking courses unrelated to his goal, despite the pleadings of his poverty stricken parents to whom he was a cruel burden.[8] Years later Freud was just as indifferent to complaints that his treatments were altogether too long and too expensive.

Contrast this with Jung's choice of medicine, and eventual specialization in psychiatry. His parents too were poor, though not as poverty stricken as Freud's. Jung decided to become a physician after sober reflection, attracted by the combination of the biological and spiritual in a physician's work. He was little if any burden on his parents and financed much of his medical education by acting as his aunt's agent in disposing of her valuable antiques.

Jung was undecided upon a specialty, leaning toward surgery if anything and indifferent to psychiatry, as the "lectures and clinical demonstrations had not made the slightest impression on me," and the cases he had seen only aroused his "boredom and disgust."[9]

In preparing for his state examinations he "attacked" Krafft-Ebing's textbook with a somewhat condescending "let's see what a psychiatrist has to say for himself" attitude, for in that day psychiatrists were not highly esteemed. Knowledge of psychiatry was limited; it was practiced in isolated asylums on the fringes of the city.

Jung became fascinated with Krafft-Ebing's observation that psychiatry was incomplete and "psychiatric textbooks are stamped with a more or less subjective character." When he read a few lines further that the psychoses could be classified as diseases of the personality, he confessed that his heart pounded so hard he was forced to stand and draw a deep breath. The intense excitement brought on a flash of "illumination that for me the only possible goal was psychiatry," because it combined both his biologi-

cal and spiritual interests. He further surmised that
psychiatric texts became subjective confessions of their
authors and psychiatrists respond to personality disorders
"with the totality of his personality and life experience,"
and that was the secret of psychiatry. It was this insight
that enabled Jung to understand Freud as no other man
would.

When this blond, genial giant called, in 1906, Freud
immediately saw him as manna from the psychiatric
heavens. Not only was Jung fascinated by Freud's
dreamology but also by his personality. They conversed
for thirteen hours, forging the bonds of friendship. Jung
soon became another Fliess, for on April 16, 1909 Freud
affectionately wrote him:

> "It is remarkable that on the same evening that
> I formally adopted you as an eldest son, annointing
> you as my successor and Crown Prince . . . that
> then and there you should have divested me of my
> paternal dignity and that the divestment seems to
> have given you as much pleasure as investing your
> personality gave me."[10]

Another compelling attraction Jung possessed was his
Christian origin as Freud believed psychoanalysis was
tainted with an overly Jewish flavor. He was indifferent
about his own Judaic origins, mocked the dietary laws
and consented only half heartedly to a Jewish marriage
ceremony. Yet, after Jung departed, the Freudians vilified
him as anti-Semitic despite both his willingness to risk
a Jewish affiliation, and his loyal defense of Freud against
discrimination. Possibly Jung did develop some such bias
later but initially he regarded the Viennese only as "Bohemian."[11] Many of these early followers were a seedy lot,
attracted more by Freud's sexology than his science and
they sensed the opportunities for exploiting popular superstitions through dream interpretations and sexual mon-
gering.

When Hanns Sachs[12] complained of one such sexually
obsessed follower who bored the Wednesday night meetings with analyses of toilet graffiti and other obscenities,

Freud agreed he was a sexual monomaniac, but asked Sachs' indulgence because "there are many highly esteemed professors and scholars who think and act in all sorts of shabby and mean ways . . . why should we be so severe with this poor devil who is no worse than they are just because he lays himself open to sneers by his sincerity?"

Apparently Freud could forgive anything of anyone subscribing to his sexual theories. Renouncing belief in their verity was the unforgiveable sin. Jung eventually aroused that animus, but at first everything was quite rosy and Freud ordained him as his "Crown Prince." Unfortunately this aroused the anti-Christian prejudices of the Viennese who rebelled against accepting Jung as their director and overseer. Although Freud's will prevailed and Jung did direct the movement for about two years, the seething hate and jealousy of the Viennese group began undermining Jung's position.

Meeting privately with Freud during a conclave in Geneva during Jung's first tenure, they conversed amicably despite the undercurrent of opposition and muttered predictions of Jung's defection by his enemies. Despite them, Jung agreed to continue as director, to Freud's intense gratification. So faithful a disciple would assure his name would be emblazoned as the greatest in metapsychology. In a glow of warmth, they parted with the promise to renew their conversation later that day. But several hours later when they resumed talking with Ernest Jones present, the old tormenting fears of defection again assailed Freud.

Jones may have planted these misgivings for he was a meddlesome personality who resented Jung's favor at court. Jones had insinuated Jung was an anti-Semitic self seeker who would renounce the sexual dogma, and his insinuations were having their affect. The conversation began assuming an ominous tone. Freud then demanded:

"Why have you not mentioned my name in your last paper?"

Jung replied rather indifferently that he thought that unnecessary as his name was "so well known."

Freud's sensitive psychic antenna got the signal — a death wish! He fainted away. Taking him in his powerful arms, Jung placed him on a couch. Coming to, Freud muttered:

"How sweet it is to die."

From that time, he took to predicting his demise. He first prognosticated he would die in his fifties; after that in his sixties. Cancer was discovered in his jaw at sixty-six. He lived another seventeen years.

A year after the fainting episode, Jung's tenure again came up for vote, with Freud supporting and the Viennese bloc opposing. As they could not reverse Jung's majority, the Viennese spitefully abstained from voting.

As Jones was a leader of the opposition, Jung derided: "And you call yourself a Christian!"

Jones tried to give the remark an anti-Semitic twist but to Freud's credit, he interpreted it as a rebuke for abandoning Christian notions of fair play. At any rate, Jung was not a very good politician, nor was he very anxious to become Freud's Crown Prince. When he soft pedalled Freud's sexology, it brought the inevitable rift.

They say Freud was never psychoanalyzed, but that is not entirely true. Jung came as close as humanly possible to that feat during their period of intimacy and mutual admiration. In their first meeting, though admittedly befuddled by "hesitations and doubts," Jung confessed deferring to what he believed was Freud's superior experience.

Freud only brushed off such doubts, attributing them to Jung's "lack of experience." For a time, Jung suppressed his skepticism but remembering Krafft-Ebing's first lesson in psychiatry, he began pondering the subjective factors which made Freud's "sexual theory enormously important to him, both personally and philosophically." He was mystified as to how much his "sexuality was connected with subjective prejudices of his, and to what extent it rested upon verifiable experience."[13]

Jung also divined that Freud was emotionally involved in his sexual theory to an extraordinary degree. When he spole of it, Jung observed that "his tone became urgent, almost anxious and all signs of his normally critical and skeptical manner vanished. A strange, deeply moved expression came over his face, the cause of which I was at a loss to understand. I had a strong intuition that for him his sexuality was a sort of *numinosum*."[14]

Jung defined *numinosum* as "Rudof Otto's *Idea of the Holy,* for the inexpressible, mysterious, terrifying, directly experienced and pertaining only to the divinity."

Jung also vividly recalled how Freud implored him:

" 'My dear Jung, promise me never to abandon the sexual theory. That is the most essential of all. You see, we must make a dogma of it, an unshakable bulwark.' He said that to me with great emotion, in the tone of a father saying: 'And promise me this one thing, my dear son, that you will go to church every Sunday.' "

Before boarding ship for their voyage to Clark University, Jung's doubts of Freud's emotional stability increased after they attended a luncheon in Bremen. When Jung conversed about some well preserved corpses that had been found in the acid laden peat bogs of the region and believed to be of prehistoric men, Freud became annoyed at his continued references to the corpses, and interrupted him several times. Then he suddenly fainted. After coming around, Freud confessed that he had interpreted Jung's continued references to the corpses as death wishes against him.

"I was more than surprised by this interpretation (and) alarmed by the intensity of his fantasies — so strong that obviously they caused him to faint," Jung related in his autobiography.

Aboard ship, they whiled away the time interpreting each other's dreams. It was a reciprocal psychoanalysis, conducted without a couch, man to man, or eyeball to eyeball, as the saying goes. When Freud presented a dream for interpretation Jung asked for more details from his

personal life. That request, Jung noticed, evoked a
"curious look — a look of the utmost suspicion. Then he
said 'But I cannot risk my authority.' At that moment
he lost it altogether . . . the end of our relationship was
already foreshadowed. Freud was placing personal authority above truth."

It was the *numinosum* again, this time bound up with
authority, a touchy word to Jung.

When their ship approached America, Jung related
to his biographer, E. A. Bennett that Freud exclaimed:

"Won't they get a surprise when they hear what we
have to say to them?"

Jung replied: "How ambitious you are."

"Me?" Freud asked. "I'm the most humble of men and
the only man who isn't ambitious."

"That's a big thing, to be the only one," Jung sarcastically replied.

Unfortunately, Jung's analysis of Freud fizzled.
Though he came very close, he failed in his greatest case;
he had not fully applied Krafft-Ebing's postulate on the
subjective factors to determine the basis of Freud's sexology. In his obituary on Freud, Jung wrote he had been
"permitted a deep glimpse into the mind of this remarkable man . . . possessed by a daemon — a man who had
been vouchsafed an overwhelming revelation that took
possession of his soul and never let him go."

The daemon, or *numinosum* which had invaded
Freud's psyche was responsible for his many violent
estrangements and his overwhelming ambition. Not even
Jung with his immense clinical experience dared guess
how this *numinosum* became formed or how it motivated
Freud. It was in fact, based on an event so incredible,
so unusual, so remote from human experience, it could
never have been guessed. It must be authenticated by
unimpeachable evidence.

## CHAPTER THREE

# Undisputed Favorite

*"A man who has been the undisputed favorite of his mother, keeps for life the feeling of a conqueror, that confidence of success that frequently induces real success."*

Just as a paleontologist constructs an entire skeleton from a single bone, Freud's complete case history can be drawn from this singular admission. Written in a moment of conscious reflection rather than vagrant free associations, its clarity mocks his claims to clairvoyancy through interpreting dreams and other unconscious phenomena.

Thinkers are usually inspired by other thinkers; learning derives from learning; science from science. With Freud it was otherwise; his inspiration arose from the undisputed (and unfair) favoritism of his mother. She lavished her boundless affection upon her "goldener Sigi" into his seventies; for she lived until ninety-six.

As her first born at only twenty, Sigmund would naturally enjoy her exclusive affection until the arrival of other children. However, he never did relinquish his advantage and if anything, her worship increased despite six following children, each of whom duplicated their mother's adulation for her first born.

In reading Freud, it is imperative to read between the lines. His statement could also be interpreted:

"A woman who foolishly marries a man old enough to be her father who soon after marriage becomes a failure, will seek solace in her children to compensate for her poor marriage."

Amalia Freud's love was also loaded with hope; hope that Sigmund would sanctify her marriage through his genius and also rescue her family from the poverty her aging husband was helpless to alleviate. It was a heavy obligation and may account for Freud's serious, worrisome nature throughout his life.

The midwife assisting at his birth predicted he would become a great man and her prediction was continually dinned into Sigmund's young ears. At three, he promised his parents he would buy them a new bedcover after he became rich and famous, to replace one he had soiled through incontinence. Over two decades later, under the spell of the same anticipation, he gleefully wrote his fiancee that he had destroyed all his notes, correspondence and diaries to confound his future biographers, thus compounding vanity with spite.[1]

At each of his mother's confinements, Sigmund experienced acute anxiety, both for the loss of her attention and dread lest she install the new child as favorite. In his maturity, Freud confessed that he had wished so fervently for the death of an infant brother who followed him but soon died, that for a long time he believed his death wishes had killed him. His swooning when he imagined Jung harbored death wishes against him, indicate how terrifying and persistent Freud's childhood superstitions remained.

Though each confinement temporarily robbed Sigmund of his mother's love, as a first born male he had little need to fear being usurped. The only serious threat to his favoritism came from a sister several years younger who showed signs of musical talent. By severe scrimping, a piano for her was managed but her triumph was short lived. Complaining that her practicing disturbed his studying, Sigmund issued an ultimatum: Either the piano left or he would.[2] Meekly, his parents bowed and his sister lost her chance for a musical education. If her talent could have brought in no more than a teacher's earnings, it would have helped the family substantially, but the undisputed favorite was too jealous to consider that. He disposed of a rival by using the power over his parents he sensed was absolute because so much hope was invested in his future success.

Basically, Freud was an unpleasant person. Except for his first three or four years when his father was comparatively wealthy, the family's circumstances were bleak. The syrupy accounts of his dedicated strivings do not hide the dull, drab, undertones of his life. Grinding poverty was always present; relatives were often begged for assistance.

Consequently Freud lived on his future hopes, conditioning himself to endure the pain of waiting for fame and glory. As a schoolboy, he was the typical grind, immersed in dry as dust studies which his phenomenal photographic memory retained after but one reading. His future occupation as paid listener to endless, boring trivia was not only painless for Freud but also enjoyable for it brought into play his phenomenal memory.

The "feeling of a conqueror" he boasted, derived from his domination of the family's love; even his father kowtowed to him. Freud was ruthless when opposed, as are all conquerors. When his interpretations were disputed, he called it "resistance," a war-like term. Freud was always at war; at war with the society that denied his genius; with colleagues who scorned his ideology and with rival schools of psychology. Sometimes he even warred with himself. In the moments of sober reflection emerging during his famous correspondence with Fliess, he sometimes rejected his own ideas. These rejections were only temporary swings of mood; his self-skepticism could never triumph permanently over the greedy ambitions his mother had inspired.

His mother's over fondness had another, even more ghastly consequence in prematurely stirring Sigmund sexually through her fondling and caressing. He confessed having his "libido" aroused (experiencing an erection) from seeing his mother in the nude at the age of three or four.

As his mother's unwitting sexual stimulation was accompanied by her cooing of future glories, ambition and sexuality were simultaneous stirrings. Two powerful but incompatible urges, sensuality and the will to power had to be reconciled. An ambitious man cannot allow sensuality to interfere with his plans; a libertine cannot allow duty to interfere with his pleasure. Freud's ingenuity in reconciling these conflicting impulses is the story of his life.

The Freud home reeked with sex, for their poverty permitted Sigmund's parents little other pleasure and his father was a potent man. In their confined quarters, Sigmund could witness the "primal scene" from his cradle in his parent's bedroom. Freud was often prone to interpret from a patient's dream material that he had witnessed parental intercourse during his infancy. Since he confessed that he found it "uncanny when I can't understand someone in terms of myself," it is not unwarranted to suspect Freud's deductions were based on his own life experience rather than the patient's.

When a patient's case history coincided with his own, this corroboration would be seized upon avidly. Since Freud has also been detected by Bernfeld[3] disguising his own case material as a patient's in "Screen Memories," it is conjectural which of his writings pertained to patients or were products of his continual self absorption.

Probably the most remarkable and detailed case history Freud ever published appeared in *Moses and Monotheism*[4] when he was almost eighty. Just why he considered this unique case suitable for inclusion in his last complete book is mystifying as it bears little relation to his theme — questioning the racial derivation of Moses.

According to Freud, the patient had severe sexual and temperamental difficulties. He could recall watching parental intercourse from his cradle in their bedroom. As his family was poor, he continued to sleep there for years, and constantly peeked and became so sensitive to his parent's stirrings that he would waken instantly to revel in the spectacle. Eventually he became an insomniac from habitually fighting off sleep to indulge his voyeurism.

Then he learned how to stimulate himself. Caught in masturbation by his mother, he was threatened with castration. This was so terrifying, he refrained from touching his penis, until he lost sensitivity in the organ. Even with the onset of puberty's powerful sexual urge, his penis remained insensitive. He could induce orgasm only through fantasies, or as Freud termed it, "psychic orgasm."

Fantasy alone constituted his sex life for the patient was timid and did not know how to approach women. The patient was also described as being very difficult, cold and demanding. He had taken up a profession he disliked to spite his father. All in all, he presented the standard, stereotyped case, the only one Freud recognized in his precious psychoanalysis, complete with castration terror, masturbating in infancy, witnessing the primal scene, father hatred, etc.

Like the case of a purported University instructor identified as Freud himself by Bernfeld[5], Freud's case study in *Moses and Monotheism* is too similar to his own to overlook. He was almost eighty at the writing. Also considering that both his age and intense suffering with cancer could have affected his sense of reality, to say nothing of the tendency to fantasy that Jung had observed, he could have dreamed up a composite case or simply become autobiographical to perpetuate his delusion. Freud's inability to detect the fantasies of parental seduction presented by his patients could also have affected his ability to separate his own fantasies from fact.

In Freud's last summary of his Oedipus theory,[6] he wrote that after learning masturbation, it is a universal lust of the man child to possess his mother "physically in the ways he has divined from his observations and intuitive surmises of sexual life and (he) tries to seduce her by showing her the male organ of which he is the proud owner."

In this phantasmagoria, Freud's amorality is obvious, for in these few words, he attributes voyeurism ("divining

from his observations") masturbation, mother incest,
exhibitionism in infants, and parricidal impulses to
eliminate fathers as love rivals. The boy of "two or three"
so described displays a precocious depravity impossible
in an undeveloped child, and possible only in a freak.
Such freaks of precocious development are known in
endocrinology; boys of three with completely developed
sexual powers including secretion of semen, are on record,
but they live only a few years.

Freud was undoubtedly extremely precocious mentally
and probably physically as well. His appetites were vor-
acious; his capacity for work and effort phenomenal.
Everything in his nature bordered on the pathological,
far beyond the usual range. For example, he smoked cigars
continually, consuming about twenty per day. He laughed
once when a friend to whom he had offered a cigar declined
because he had just finished one. Evidently he could not
comprehend why anyone could not instantly smoke
another just as he did.

Freud's subjective involvement determined his every
tenet just as Krafft-Ebing maintained. The universal case
of Oedipal motivations he postulated, was in reality only
an anomaly, as was Freud himself. Moreover so unusual
a person, dedicated from birth to striving for the utmost
heights, endowed with almost unbelievable energy, was
capable of actions far beyond the usual range of human
behavior. Only a man with an enormous ego could set
himself up as the supreme authority in psychology behol-
den to no one because in his egomania he believed his
system was completely independent and autonomous.
Since Freud postulated that all human behavior is based
upon sexual conditioning, it predicates the possibility that
his intellectual megalomania had a sexual counterpart.

The fact that Freud was born of a mother whose husband was old enough to be her father, alone set him apart
for such marriages are unusual. His parents union resem-
bled an incestual relationship; it was therefore somewhat
tainted. In his eyes, if such a relationship was permissible,
then his lust for his mother was equally permissible, par-

ticularly since she had stimulated his desire through her caresses and her undisputed favoritism indicated she regarded him like a lover. In his contributions to sexuality, Freud maintained that a mother's love for her children is a reciprocal sexual relationship.[7]

Such distorted thinking, originating in his childhood, could certainly have culminated in a bizarre, wild act. How wild it was defies the imagination, for it is an act that probably has no precedent since primitive man, if then.

As I have mentioned, one of the autobiographical incidents Freud recounted which stuck in my memory, was his urinating in his parents' bedroom. He conveyed the impression that he did it impulsively though Jones and Fromm contend it was deliberate, without justifying their contention.

Whether impulsive or deliberate, when it occurred his father was so incensed he growled:

"This boy will never amount to anything."

Years later the "boy" wrote in his masterpiece:

"This must have been a terrible affront to my ambitions for allusions to this scene recur again and again in my dreams and are constantly coupled with enumerations of my accomplishments and successes, as though I wanted to say, 'You see, I have amounted to something after all.' "

Freud's willingness to plead guilty to disrespect by urinating in his parents bedroom, would be comparable to pleading guilty to a misdemeanor whereas the felony was really murder in the first degree. Actually, he had urinated in the throes of an uncontrollable terror, a terror and fear that continued to haunt him throughout his traumatic life. The memory of his trauma probably constitutes the nucleus of the *numinosum* which Jung suspected as the root of his sexual dogma.

From Freud's own unpublished memoranda, this is what really happened, as resurrected by Irving Stone in his *Passions of the Mind:*[9]

"One night when he was seven years old, he had gone into his parents' bedroom ... the door had been firmly closed though not locked. As he stepped into the darkness of the room there had been a series of movements in his parents' bed, dimly seen and heard, and not understood, which upset him terribly. His father sensing that someone was in the room, had turned his head over his shoulder to look back, seen the boy standing there and subsided in whatever he was doing. The next scene was hazy in Sigmund's mind; sometimes he saw himself urinating on floor just inside the door, at other times he had a blurred impression of having run to the bed, thrown himself into his mother's arms and micturated there. His father was so disgusted that he had said:

" 'The boy will come to nothing.' "

Tenderly, his mother soothed him and carried him to his bed. According to Stone, Freud was deeply ashamed of his act and in pondering on his motivation, concluded:

"He had been jealous of his father! *He had wanted to interrupt and put a stop to what was going on!* (Italics Stone's) . . . to oust his father . . . completing the love act which he had surprised in process?"

Stone's saccharine explanation for Freud's monstrous intrusion is not compatible with the man's amoral, perverse character. He could not admit guilt or fault because a genius cannot be wrong. Nor can an intensely ambitious, egomanic personality ever admit error. The blow to his self esteem when his father angrily predicted he would never amount to anything was undoubtedly traumatic.

Freud's primal scene can be reconstructed far more realistically, considering his inordinate jealousy. While lying in bed that night, after possibly sensing his father's eagerness to retire, his jealousy was compounded with a terror that a new rival for his mother's affection might be conceived that night. His father's ability to delight his mother beyond his childish powers could also have convulsed him.

Unable to contain himself when he heard their stirrings, he burst into their room as his parents were about to

assume the primal position. Leaping into their bed to in-
terpose himself between them, he discharged the only fluid
possible from the "little organ of which he was the proud
possessor." Growling like an animal in pain, his father
may have tried to seize him but his mother tenderly inter-
vened, kissing and fondling him as she carried him back to
his bed, believing he had had a nightmare.

The next day, amnesia developed except for the fact
that he had urinated in his parents' bedroom. Years later,
during his self analysis Freud probably penetrated his own
amnesia and reconstructed the entire incident and even
made notes. It was of course impossible to reveal all the
circumstances of his primal scene, so he mentioned only
his father's angry remark. Unable to whip him, his father
struck a telling psychic blow by attempting to demolish his
mother's worshipping faith in his future fame and riches.

Reviewing Freud's life in the light of this traumatic
event, leads to the conclusion he never completely recovered his poise. The confidence of a conqueror instilled by
his mother, was coupled with terror of the failure his
father predicted. The slightest hint that he was not infalli-
ble, that his views were questionable, that he was not an
immortal genius, revived the panic he had experienced
that night and could account for his savage hatred of dissidents and critics.

To counteract that terror, he was forced to strain every
nerve toward attaining greatness to succeed beyond all the
family's dreams and expectations, by attaining the impossible. Only by superhuman efforts could he stave off doom
and ignominy. His father must be proved wrong; totally,
ridiculously, stupidly and blindly wrong.

Freud's sex life was traumatically affected. His attempt at sexual fulfillment under such grotesque circumstances, deterred him from further attempts. Like the case
he described, he did not know how to approach a woman
and probably satisfied himself through psychic onanism.

Thus far, Freud's sex mania, his blatant egotism, his
propensity for meddling and snooping originating in voyeurism, his lust for power, his terror of challenges, his

death wish theory and Oedipal manifestations have been
traced to his childhood origins. Every one of his shib-
boleths, such as penis envy of women, never substantiated
clinically and strongly opposed, may also have originated
then. During playing with his Uncle John, and a little girl
cousin, both about his age, possibly the two boys competed
one day in a peeing contest. The little girl, shut off from the
sport, may have squealed in envy and disappointment. In
maturity, Freud hinted of his recurring feelings of guilt
about this little girl because of sexual liberties taken with
her. Later, Freud sprang his penis envy theory upon the
world in his search for an idea that had never occurred to
anyone else based on his some such childhood incident or
material from a seance. Only a few observations or disclosures sufficed to enable Freud to spin an elaborate
theory.

Another shibboleth, hailed as an immortal discovery
really originated with Boerne, an obscure philosopher of
the early nineteenth century, who advised aspiring writers to jot down every idea that crossed their minds, quickly
and spontaneously. After a few days of such practice, he
predicted they would be astonished by their production.

Freud's superb literary style, his most solid gift, with
his amazing fluidity is ample testimony to the merit of
Boerne's advice, easily recognizable as the inspiration for
the "free association of ideas." But encouraging random,
undirected talk, stretches analyses to inordinate lengths,
spares the analyst from eliciting pertinent facts or even
discussing the products of free associations. Obviously,
pursuing a significant disclosure may lead to the root of
the neurosis and terminate it, and his fees as well.

Freud's disrespect for authority, for the rights of privacy, for the sanctity of human relationships, can be traced
to the incongruous marriage of his parents, legal of course
but unsanctified by deep love. Consequently Freud fan-
tasied another, more romantic family of his birth, based on
wish rather than fact. As a child of two or three, he had
mistaken a half brother about his mother's age, as his
father and was deeply disappointed when he learned the

truth.

Anal eroticism is another shibboleth of the Freudian faith, easily accounted for. When Sigmund learned his mother became concerned when he failed to have a movement, he was delighted at her concern and deliberately withheld or delayed defecation. The Freudians have spun some very elaborate interpretations based on anal eroticism and the retention of fecal matter. It is an insane idea; no person with the slightest knowledge of hygiene would constipate himself. But in a child, abnormally craving demonstrations of his mother's concern and affection, it is very possible. This perverse idea may also account for Freud's demands for ever lengthening analyses for the longer he kept people under his sway, the longer they would demonstrate their love and affection, (transference.)

On consulting his family circumstances and the concentration of admiration, affection and worship lavished upon him by all the members of his family, it is apparent that Freud eventually became addicted to demonstrations of admiration. He could not tolerate anything except blind obedience from his disciples. It was the same adulation his family had bestowed upon him early in life which became an indispensible need.

## CHAPTER 4

# Improper Physician

*"After forty-one years of medical activity, my self knowledge tells me that I have never been a physician in the proper sense."*

Freud's impulsive, abrupt decision to study medicine, could have been prompted by several converging desires, to learn why he had so madly intruded upon his parents, or to dissolve his sexual obsession which he sensed endangered his hopes of success, or simply to indulge his voyeurist tendencies through the intimacies permitted a physician.

His career at the University of Vienna has been covered so minutely, repeating a few highlights from those years should suffice. They were thirteen years of grinding poverty, incessant diligence, striving, dreaming, writing and scheming, while his parents suffered in poverty. In all his writings, Freud never expressed a word of gratitude for their sacrifices. Had he been concerned about his family's poverty, he could have entered practice five or six years before he eventually did at thirty.

His decision to leave the University was forced upon him both by the bleakness of his prospects for a faculty appointment and his urge to marry. In his last years at the University Freud was separated from his fiancee most of the time, but his correspondence afforded much opportunity to exercise his literary gifts in effusions similar to his rhapsody on Sir Rider Haggard's *She*. His letters were merely exercises in lavish expressions of tenderness. The object of his affections, a timid, passive girl, dutifully saved them all for posterity. One letter to her was twenty-eight pages long, a release for Freud's volcanic stores of energy. Most letters dwelt on his work, dreams and plans. His gleeful boast to her of destroying his memoranda to confound his future biographers, has already been cited.

Despite his minuscule capacity for affection, Freud's adulants have romanticized his courtship to nauseous lengths. According to Ernest Jones:[1]

"Freud's attitude toward the loved one was far from one of simple attraction. It was a veritable *grande passion* . . . the terrible power of love with all its raptures fears and torments . . . all the passions of his intense nature. If ever a fiery apprenticeship qualified a man to discourse authoritatively on love, that man was Freud."

The truth is that Freud's courtship was attended with sickening displays of jealousy, tantrums and petty squabbling. He tried to alienate his fiancee from her mother, and also instigated a feud with his future brother-in-law, Eli, who was also courting his own sister. It was a miracle he did not sabotage his sister's marriage prospects, as he had her musical education. His future mother-in-law tried to break up both engagements and moved the family to Hamburg to get away from the Freuds.

Imagine a man deeply in love, writing to his future bride about her mother in this fashion:

"She is fascinating, but alien, and will always remain so to me . . . Her very warm heartedness has an air of condescension, and she exacts admiration. I can foresee more than one opportunity of making myself disagreeable to her and I don't intend to avoid them."

This cold blooded, spiteful attitude provides a glimpse of the emotional make-up of the future master psychoanalyst. Nothing was ever sacred to this man. He could brook no rivalry whatsoever, not even a daughter's love and respect for her own mother.

Mrs. Bernays, the object of his spite, was a woman of fine discernment. When Freud insisted with offensive petulance on immediate marriage despite an impending call up for one month's military service, his future mother-in-law rebuked him from Hamburg:

"First regain some calmness and peace of mind which at present is so entirely wrecked. You have no reason whatever for your ill humor and despondency which borders on the pathological . . . become once more a sensible *man*. At the moment you are like a spoilt *child* who can't get his own way and cries, believing in that way he can get everything."[2]

Psychiatry lost a wonderful prospect in Mama Bernays. In diagnosing Freud's emotions as "pathological" she evinced insight, surpassing most of his professional associates.

Freud himself was not immune from remorse in his saner moments. "You are waiting for a not very agreeable man," he once wrote his fiancee, "but I hope one who will give you no cause for regret."[3]

His irritability can be traced to the recurring anxiety he underwent each time his mother's confinements robbed him of her tender solicitude. In one remarkable passage in his "Three Contributions to the Theory of Sex," he acknowledged that a mother can prematurely excite her child's sexual instinct with excessive love until the child cannot bear being deprived of it, or having to share it with others in the family.

Freud's tendency for gloomy exaggerations betrayed him when his month of military service loomed. He growled and complained about losing valuable time, but after it was over according to Irving Stone, another official biographer, he enjoyed living in the open, friendship with his comrades and found his medical experience valuable in his later practice.

According to Jones, this too had once excited his dread as he "contemplated with an increasingly heavy heart the unescapable decision of leaving his laboratory work for the practice of medicine." These forebodings were just as groundless, even though his advent into practice was not immediately successful and income only came slowly. His forbidding personality can be blamed for his inability to build a practice despite the many advantages he otherwise possessed, such as an excellent bearing and appearance and his fine though unappreciated training at the greatest medical teaching center in the world of that day.

Another little appreciated boon was the help and guidance of Josef Breuer, a man of infinite kindness and generosity. His benefactions included financial help, referrals of patients but most valuable, an introduction to hypnotic therapy. For the few years of his association with Breuer, Freud attained some success and satisfaction in practicing hypnotism and acknowledged he was flattered by the awe he aroused.

Freud collaborated with Breuer in their *Studies on Hysteria*,[4] but it is almost impossible to believe after reading his contribution, that psychoanalysis emerged from the same man, strongly suggesting that only profound changes in personality accompanied its fabrication.

One strong influence affecting Freud, was the power he could exercise through suggestion and hypnotism, feeding both his theatrical temperament and his fervor to "amount to something." His latent sexual obsessions had also been stirred by Charcot's revelations of sexual maladjustment in nervous illnesses.[5] Sexual investigations therefore promised to satisfy two passionate yens, one for immortality through an astounding discovery in sexology and the other for limitless probing into sexual intimacies.

In 1893 Freud published "A Case of Successful Treatment by Hypnotism," [6] which provides a pre-view of his future tactics. Three years previously, a young mother whom he had known since their school days, had been unable to nurse her first born child. She became so agitated at every attempt she was forced to engage a wet nurse.

With the birth of a second child and the recurrence of the same symptoms, her physicians, Breuer and Lott,

referred her to Freud. He successfully induced hypnotism
on his first call and enabled the woman to nurse her child.
His description of the patient's symptoms were competent
and professional until Freud lapsed into a complaint that
"far from being welcomed as a saviour in the hour of
need," he was received with "bad grace" and a lack of
confidence.

However, the first good response faded after the heavy
midday meal next day. Freud returned in the evening,
again induced hypnosis and then with an incredible lack
of tact, suggested that she break out against her family
"with some acrimony" by demanding her dinner querul-
ously and asking if they meant "to let her starve;" how
then could she feed her baby, etc.

And despite his unprofessional, unethical form of suggestion, it worked and the woman could nurse her baby.
With incredible blindness to his own tactics, Freud mentioned in his paper that her husband had thought it queer
that his wife had demanded food so crassly, with remonst-
rations quite unusual for her. Relapsing again into pique,
Freud wrote he found "it hard to understand that no reference was ever made to my remarkable achievement."

Evidently Freud brooded about his lack of appreciation
and continued hoping his services would be required at
the woman's next confinement. "My time came a year
later," he gloated for the woman again failed in nursing
her next baby and he was again called. Again Freud
induced hypnotism and achieved the same happy result.

On this occasion, however, Freud discussed the case
brilliantly, attributing the woman's disability to her
strenuous attempt to exercise will power which only
defeated her purpose. He diagnosed her disability as "hys-
terique d'occasion" brought on by powerful emotional factors.

At that time, Freud induced patients to recall under
hypnosis. Later, he merely placed his hand on the brow
and commanded remembrance of painful memories in
association with some symptom to trace its origin. This
technique was quick and effective, traumatic memories

came to the surface with subsequent beneficial abreactions, he reported.

These methods, however, were derived from hypnotism and suggestion which made Freud a mere worker in an established field. His unbridled ambition to be an innovator, to make the great discovery, left him discontented. When his sexual obsessions became aroused, he concentrated upon the sexual as the sole cause of trauma, only to encounter decided repugnance and ridicule. The first casualty was Breuer, his friend and mentor to whom he owed so much, including a substantial financial obligation. When Breuer gagged at swallowing his sexual monomania, he aroused all the hatred and venom Freud could exude. Breuer's many kindnesses meant nothing once he touched Freud's super sensitive *numinosum*.

Freud's period of "splendid isolation" then began, supposedly the most agonized, tormented years of his life. The instant fame and fortune so confidently expected only continued to elude him; ostracism and ridicule was his bitter lot. As his frustration mounted, he became feverish and overwrought. In this state, psychoanalysis was born.

Occasionally Freud emerged from his frenetic concentration capable of repudiating ideas once espoused with a holy fervor. These swings from fanatic belief to cool skepticism, imposed a fearful strain on his nervous system, remarkable though it was. In Freud's fascinating correspondence with Wilhelm Fliess during their scientific love affair, the dangerous swings from belief to disbelief were continually manifested.

Though the two correspondents were similar personalities, Fliess dominated. He was abler and shrewder than Freud, and in much better circumstances both through an advantageous marriage and a lucrative practice. Freud never overawed him; toward the end of their scientific love affair, indications are that he ridiculed Freud to the verge of contempt. Neither were distinguished by a fine sense of honor or burdened by high ethical standards. Their scientific love affair ended in a sickening squabble and mutual betrayal.

Freud's first letter to Fliess typified his monumental gall for he confided that he intended to favor Charcot in his controversy over hypnotism with Bernheim, whose book he was then engaged in translating. He also impudently flayed Professor Meynert, a respected authority on neurology, for talking "authoritatively on a subject of which he knew nothing."

A year later though complaining of feeling isolated, inert and stagnant, Freud confessed that when "you thought something of me, I actually started thinking something of myself and the picture of confident energy which you offered was not without its effect." He further lamented upon the low state of learning in Vienna where for years he had been unable to find instruction.

Evidently only Freud could teach Freud. The teaching soon became sexually oriented and his letters dealt almost exclusively with his probings of the sex lives of his patients, who he boasted sometimes exclaimed:

"No one has ever asked me that before."

Anxiety over his dwindling practice, attributable to the intimate questions only he asked, became compounded with fatigue and tension. This brought on cardiac symptoms in 1894, attended with depression, gloomy visions of impending death and a waning of his remarkable diligence. However, he then confided fatuously, that when he rested, good health and spirits partially revived.

Once rested, the same dizzy swings from panic and fears of failure to the ecstacy of anticipating glorious success kept recurring. Both adverse and favorable omens spurred him on. Criticism aroused the same bitter resentment as his father's angry retort he would never "amount to anything;" favorable signs and omens such as a crowded waiting room or productive thinking meant his goal could be attained with a little extra push.

"I have the distinct feeling that I have touched on one of the greatest secrets of nature," he exulted. In an opposite swing, he dolefully predicted a fiasco when his theory of the neuroses became published.

He dreaded some other worker would anticipate his

discovery. Severe anxiety overcame him when Moebius announced a new book on hysteria, which was followed by intense relief because sexuality was not involved. He also confessed picking up Janet's new work with a painfully beating heart only to lay it down with his pulse normal. Janet, too, he gloated, had overlooked the all important sexual clues.

He worked at a fearful pace, only halting his speculations on the nature of neuroses when his tired brain produced absurdities or complete exhaustion set in, as it did almost every day for several months in 1895. Suddenly he became obsessed that dreams could solve the enigma of hysteria, confiding:

"For two whole weeks I was in a fever of writing and thought I had found the secret, but now I know I have not got it yet."

Four days later his brain glowed again, and he exulted:

"One strenuous night when I was in the stage of painful discomfort in which my brain works best, the barriers suddenly lifted, the veils dropped and it was possible to see from the details of neurosis all the way to the very conditioning of consciousness. Everything fell into place, the cogs meshed, the thing really seemed to be a machine which in a moment would run of itself."

But when Fliess' answering letter arrived a healthy reaction set in. Freud was amazed to discover his friend was an even greater "visionary" than himself for in the meantime, the machine so perfectly visualized only four days before, had stalled. As the old doubts again invaded his mind, he hoped that his daily practice would confirm his theories. A few days later, after presenting three lectures on hysteria in a confessed impudent manner, he was again his cocky, arrogant self. When his fame finally arrived, arrogance became a fixed trait; at this stage of his life, it alternated with humility and doubt.

In May of 1896, after several more ups and downs, Freud's hopes were permanently pinned upon dreams completely overlooked by psychiatry and scientific psychology.

What a stroke of genius if he could rout gypsies and fortune
tellers and claim dreams for science. Combining sexology
with dream interpretation started the old fever for immortality all over again; sexual gibberish strewed his letters.
In a state Freud described as "dead tired yet mentally
fresh," he evolved his theories of sexuality and accepted
Fliess' notion of 23 and 28 day periodicity in sexual desire
to which he added his concepts of perversion, seduction
by fathers and erotegenic zones capable of releasing anxiety. Other weird concepts plagued him such as the broom-
sticks witches rode were really "Lord Penis;" perversions
were remnants of primitive sexual cults; all sexual perversions were alike, were meaningful and conformed to old
patterns; hysterical fantasies could originate from things
heard but not understood by infants of six or seven months.
The correlation with his own infant life when he slept
in his parents' bedroom is obvious.

Dreams became his greatest inspiration, never abandoned in his moments of greatest despair. Freud
unabashedly discerned in one of his own a lustful desire
for his own daughter; in another, paralysis while walking
upstairs indicated sexual impotence. All this was followed
by the inevitable crash when Freud became determined
to test his theories in the crucible of actual experiment.

Heretofore clinical confirmation from patients had
been disappointing. Patients were unreliable; they balked
at divulging vital information; they presented fantasies
as realities; they were squeamish, cowardly and
impatient. Needed: The ideal patient, willing to allow
unlimited access to his inner life. He finally appeared.
His name was Sigmund Freud; self analysis began.

In his first communique, Freud complained of "intellectual paralysis"; writing had become a torture; he was
plagued by odd states of mind breeding nebulous thoughts
and veiled doubts. Doubts of what? Did patient Freud
doubt his doctor's competence?

Freud was in dead earnest about his self analysis. The
feat was really "Herculean," as worshipful Ernest Jones
declared. Freud admitted his confusion and ignorance of

the psychic wheels whirling within his skull and guessed that Fliess himself was somehow involved, and that his reasoning functioned poorly and hindered attaining insight. In that summer of 1897, he realized he had tackled the most difficult experiment of his life which brought on a despondent lethargy. It was a tremendous relief to depart for his summer vacation.

Refreshed, rested and eager to face the truth, on September 21, 1897 he returned to confess immediately to Fliess "the great secret which has been slowly dawning on me in recent months. I no longer believe in my *neurotica.*"

His inability to conclude his analysis, or to hold patients he considered the most suitable subjects, or to achieve complete successes, provoked his repudiation. His partial successes could be attributed to "other, familiar ways" he acknowledged, probably meaning the suggestive influences Bernheim used so effectively. Fantasies of seduction by parents which Freud had believed, he now realized were fictions. His most startling admission was that the unconscious mind could not distinguish between fantasy and reality; nor did it hold the secrets of infantile conditioning because these secrets did not emerge in deliria. Neither would they emerge in practice, he further reasoned.

Though destroying his entire theoretical structure, Freud confessed feeling deep relief. Had he divined that his renunciation was really victory over the tyrant constantly goading him on, bringing him to the verge of disgrace, ruin and madness?

The transformation was remarkable. Freud vowed to abandon his dreams of eternal fame, wealth and freedom from care, to live modestly as a mere physician. Unfortunately, his reformation was incomplete; for in the next paragraph he reasserted faith in his "psychology," which is inexplicable for his psychology was based on the very concepts of the unconscious mind he had professed discarding in the previous paragraph.

"It is a pity one cannot live on dream interpretation,"

Freud lamented in conclusion.

Back in practice, Freud resumed his self analysis only to incur the same symptoms all over again. He gave it up a few weeks later, convinced that true self analysis was impossible because the psychic forces opposing themselves were too strong. Then buoyed up by his undying faith in dreams, now a consuming passion, he began gathering material.

With the new century, his dream studies appeared. Except for a few favorable comments, there was ominous indifference or cold, cruel reviews. Freud tried to console himself with the belief he was fifteen or twenty years ahead of his time, but his isolation and the poor response to his book were demoralizing. The "severe neurosis" which Ernest Jones suspected he had once undergone, could have seized him then. He refused another meeting with Fliess on the ground he had been "going through a deep inner crisis," and dwelling on his woes would leave him in an agitated state during the long train ride back to Vienna.

It was the nadir. Discord with Fliess began to develop. Freud then blabbed away his bi-sexual theory, which was published by Weininger and robbed Fliess of priority. Because of his own overwhelming fear of being robbed in that fashion, it was the perfect vengeance.

Fliess claimed that bad feelings erupted from "some personal animosity arising from envy in Freud's attitude to me. Freud had once said to me . . . 'It is a good thing that we are friends. I would die of envy if I heard that anyone else in Berlin was making such discoveries.' "[7]

The end of their once tender friendship with its homosexual connotations was bitter and sordid. Weininger committed suicide shortly after publishing Fliess' theories. When Fliess demanded he explain how Weininger had secured this material, Freud lied shamelessly and denied giving Weininger any help or that he had "read his book before publication." He also accused the dead man of breaking "into private property with a key he picked up by chance. That is all I know about it."

Fliess caught Freud in lie after lie until he was forced to admit "you have more right on your side then I originally thought." Then he also admitted he had read the Weininger manuscript and that he had forgotten his "own attempt to steal this idea from you." His new method of interpreting the unconscious mind now permitted him to pass off his lies as merely forgetting the truth.

Freud also asserted cynically it would have done no good to fight the plagiarism, as Weininger could claim originality. He closed his long, evasive and hypocritical explanations with a complaint that it is "not my fault if you only find the time and inclination to write to me on such a trivial matter."

A breach of trust was trivial! Now they were bitter enemies. They agreed to destroy each other's letters, but Fliess treacherously preserved Freud's. Years later they were redeemed from a Berlin bookseller. Blind to their real significance, the Freudian interests published the letters at *The Origins of Psychoanalysis*.[8] From the standpoint of vengeance, what could be sweeter to Fliess?

The depth of Freud's capacities for rancor and spite can be guaged from the necessity to suppress from his letters to Fliess his vituperative mentions of Breuer, his greatest benefactor, a man to whom he was still in debt for generous loans made during his internship and first years in practice and who had also made it possible for him to establish a practice through his referrals.

## CHAPTER 5

# The Deviations

*"I became a doctor from being compelled to deviate from my original purpose."*

Freud's situation after his break with Fliess was desperate. He was in disrepute; his practice was at a low. Youth was gone; he could no longer bear the turbulent swings from exultant anticipation to bitter disillusionment.

"For many years," Jones declaims, "he suffered from periodic depression and fatigue or apathy, neurotic symptoms which later took the form of anxiety attacks before being dispelled by his own analysis."

On the contrary, the symptoms mentioned above became intensified when Freud started self-analysis. As he also disclosed to Fliess, "True self analysis is impossible; the forces arrayed against each other are too strong." Moreover, Jones had witnessed his swooning episode with Jung, and many other displays of deep emotional disturbance during his close association with Freud, proving that his symptoms had not been "dispelled by his own analysis."

In 1909 Jung bluntly wrote Freud himself that he suffered from a neurosis. "Apparently neither Freud nor his disciples could understand what it meant for the theory and practice of psychoanalysis if not even the Master could deal with his own neurosis," Jung also wrote in his autobiography.

The point Jung missed was that Freud did deal with his own neurosis and very shrewdly. Psychoanalysis was the successful exploitation of his own Oedipal syndrome. Unfortunately he was compelled to preserve his own disturbance to exploit it just as he did with patients and could only maintain a delicate mental balance throughout his tormented life. Nor did he ever complete his self-analysis, according to Jones and reserved a specific time each day for continued introspections. Scrutiny of the evolution of Freud's technique will reveal how it solved his problems without forcing him to relinquish all the vanities, conceits, delusions, fears and voyeuristic inclinations which constituted his neurosis.

In his remarkable letter of September 21, 1897, Freud admitted his inability to complete analyses or to hold patients, and attributed his partial results to suggestion. Since his income was jeopardized through his failures, his dreams of fame and fortune would have to be jettisoned. If only he could make a living through dream interpretations, he had bemoaned in that remarkable letter to Fliess.

When psychoanalysis was finally established on a lucrative basis, all these difficulties were eliminated. Only patients contracting for hundreds of seances without any guarantee of a result, were acceptable; they could not "run away." Dream interpretations did become a way to make a living, the "via rega" to the unconscious mind. Modesty and humility were discarded for the megalomanic claim that psychoanalysis was an invaluable instrument of scientific research, entitling him to recognition as an immortal genius, the greatest of our century if not of all time. Throgh his megalomanic aversion for a physician's duties, Freud attained his "original purpose." His deviation consisted in creating a profession permitting free indulgence of his egomania.

At the nadir of his career, his most pressing need was for patients who would not "run away." One day a wealthy patient reprimanded Freud for interrupting her. Meekly,

Freud held his tongue. The woman rambled on freely and returned again and again. The lesson was not lost upon Freud; he abandoned quesioning to listen passively, thus avoiding both depleting his exhausted energies and incurring antagonisms through tactless inquiries.

Then he recalled Boerne's advice to aspiring writers and adopted it as the "free association of ideas." Patients could be encouraged through the suggestive influences he employed to blurt out everything in the hopes of securing relief, ignoring notions of the relevant, distasteful or trivial. Under the guise of treatment he secured endless material for interpretation.

The interpretation closest to his heart was Oedipal motivations, with its incestual ties and parricidal connotations. Caution had to be observed before drawing such offensive conclusions; a rapport must first be established. In his directive for securing associations for dream interpretations, Freud advised:

"As will be seen, the point is to induce a psychic
state which is in some degree analogous, as regards
the distribution of psychic energy (mobile attention)
to the state of mind before falling asleep, and also
of course to the hypnotic state."[1]

Lying on the couch could induce "the state of mind before falling asleep" which was also "in some degree analogous" to the hypnotic state. Through such phraseology, Freud hypnotized himself into believing he was not using hypnotism. These lines were composed in the dead of night, when he himself was half asleep, in the state analogous to hypnotism. In passively listening to free associations, Freud also relapsed in a semi-hypnotized condition.

His remarkable agility in skating over the thinnest ice permitted him to admit the very thing he also could deny. His double talk is most obvious in his efforts to disassociate the transference (psychoanalytic trance) from the hypnotic trance, as in this passage from his *General Introduction to Psychoanalysis:*[2]

"Now you will say, that regardless of whether the

driving force behind the analysis is called transference or suggestion, the danger still remains that our
influence upon the patient may bring the objective
certainties of our discoveries into doubt; and that
what is an advantage in therapy is harmful to
research. This is the objection that has most frequently been raised against psychoanalysis and it
must be admitted, even though it is unjustifiable,
it cannot be ignored as unreasonable."

If it cannot be ignored as unreasonable, or to put it
in positive terms, if it can be recognized as reasonable,
how can it be unjustifiable?

Actually Freud had powerful subjective reasons for
employing hypnotism, for he had won regard as a "miracle
worker," when he applied it before inventing
psychoanalysis. He also had powerful subjective reasons
for denying its use, for it thereby reduced him to the status
of a mere worker in an established field. Consequently
he deprecated hypnotism as unreliable, "reminiscent of
magic; conjuring and hocus pocus." It was mechanical
drudgery, "hodman's work'" wholly unscientific. Besides,
the hypnotic state was not always possible to induce, he
added.

Once transferred on the couch, patients were overawed by the remarkable interpretive skill of the genius
sitting behind, out of sight. The goal of the treatment
became the interpretations rendered in the glow of transference which assured blind acceptance. Suppose one
attempts to visualize how Freud the psychoanalyst could
have handled his "Successful Case of Hypnotism."

Instead of suggesting to his patient she would have
a good appetite and could nurse her child, as a psychoanalyst he could suggest or encourage her own fear that her
symptoms were serious, requiring long, careful study; that
while he could guarantee no result, he must have
unlimited access to her innermost thoughts, feelings, and
sex life; that she would be privileged to hear the interpretations of a man of science with unparalleled insight who
had founded a new metaphysics with absolutely breath-

taking possibilities, loaded with ideas and implications
no other worker had had the genius to perceive.

But he could caution his patient his ministrations must
be strictly private; they must never be discussed with
her husband or others in the family and must become
the foremost interest of her life. Criticisms of uninformed
opponents or impatient relatives must be ignored, for such
disparagements can be attributed to malice, to the prejudices of a society outraged by the truth it cowardly
refused to face — the workings of the Oedipus complex.

This is the essence of Freud's propaganda line as
strewn throughout his writings and imitated by his disciples. And it worked effectively to recruit both patients
and practitioners for a man is bound to find believers,
if he speaks long enough, loud enough and disseminates
his message widely enough. Freud's disciples were often
malcontents, dreamers and meddlers like himself. His
reasoning appealed to them. Though the derision greeting
his *Interpretations of Dreams* was a deep shock, converts
were nevertheless made. For years sales were agonizingly
slow, but there were some sales which induced the fascinated to seek him out.

From Freud's standpoint the book was indeed a masterpiece; "Inspiration such as this comes but once in a
lifetime," he boasted in his preface. Jung became con-
verted through the dreamology though finding it difficult
to assimilate at first. Hanns Sachs was a more typical
convert who discovered his mission in life after one reading. Completely naive, trusting and worshipful, Sachs rose
to the top in the hierarchy but inadvertently also contributed authentic evidence of Freud's implacable hatreds
in his insistence that his followers join his persistent
attacks on Adler, Stekel, Jung and other defectors. These
traitors must not be allowed to call themselves
psychoanalysts, he fumed, As Sachs wrote:[3]

"Freud never underestimated the importance of
psychoanalysis being known as his own brain child. He
felt convinced that it was one of the most far reaching
and fateful discoveries that man ever made on his way

to self knowledge." To keep psychoanalysis so identified, Freud "was untiring and unbending, hard and sharp like steel, a good hater close to the limit of vindictiveness."

When he found that both dream interpretations and permitting unlicensed babbling were profitable, Freud created a new profession — the paid listener. His clients were too enlightened to believe in gypsies and fortune tellers but succumbed to practically the same superstitions if they were phrased in a scientific jargon. Prospective practitioners then began flocking around Freud; some sincerely believed in his therapeutic claims; others were delighted with the easy money, with the power they could exert over their reclining subjects and with indulging their propensities for meddling and snooping.

Belief was the prime requisite; belief first, understanding will perhaps come later, Freud counselled. If instead skepticism arose as it did in Adler, then the skeptic must be ex-communicated. Most followers however, were true believers and the loss of a few skeptics was never fatal. Freud's vindictiveness toward dissenters, however, could have been due to his own underlying skepticism which became too painful to admit.

"Freud himself once said to me," Jones relates in the official tomes, "that the simplest way of learning psychoanalysis was to believe all he wrote was true and then, after understanding it, one could criticize it in any way one wished. I rejoined that credulity and denial were too near each other emotionally for the path to be a safe one."

With the years, Freud learned that it was best for him to sit out of sight of his patients. When Hanns Sachs asked him why, Freud snapped:

"Because I cannot stand being stared at ten hours a day."[4]

His real reason for sitting out of sight was to prevent patients from seeing the mocking, supercilious expression wont to him and typical of egomaniacs. From experience, he had learned his facial expressions provoked patients to "run away." Freud was aware of this obnoxious trait in himself and inadvertently revealed it in a chance discussion with a fellow train traveler on slips of the tongue. When the man's free associations encountered a psychic block, he exclaimed:

"Please don't make a mocking face as if you were gloating over my embarrassment, but help me."[5]

Freud's meddling propensities, as so overtly displayed during his betrothal, can be illustrated from another example.[6] He had forbidden a patient to see or telephone his sweetheart, but when the patient lifted the phone to call another number, he automatically asked for his sweetheart's. This proved unconscious direction, Freud triumphantly asserted; it also proved he was something of a petty tyrant and just as jealous of his patients' emotional attachments as he had once been of his own fiancee's.

When Freud discovered how easy and lucrative it was to sit back and listen, he endowed himself as a research institution. Then, by addressing himself to the public in his inimitable style, he fascinated untold thousands with his theories. Writers and playwrights incorporated his themes in their creations, thus providing free advertising and attracting more believers.

Though slow in getting there, success did arrive; psychoanalysis became a popular and fashionable means of exploiting age-old superstitions and fancies. Though some men of integrity did enlist under Freud's banner, his disciples for the most part duplicated many of his foibles, a fascination for intimacy, for prying and meddling and an inability to act in a crisis.

With the wide circulation of his books among laymen, analysis sounded valid. Clients were "sold" before consulting analysts, who were carefully instructed on how to contract for their services. In his directives[7] Freud advised screening out unsuitable cases by immediately informing all prospective clients of immense difficulties and uncertainties. This in itself was good salesmanship for it cultivated an impression of his great integrity. If later they complained of the expense without experiencing relief,

Freud callously advised reminding complainers that they had been warned about that in their first visit. Those who would not accept such conditions in their first visit, did not belong on the couch so nothing was lost. Obviously, those accepting such one-sided conditions were suggestible and therefore suitable for analysis.

Once free associations began, they could continue interminably. The discussion of one dream, one slip of the tongue or one episode, could continue for many seances. There were no short cuts; no time savers, as my own experience discloses If the patient remained mute on the couch, he was not to be prodded into talking. Nor was he to be shocked by premature interpretations of Oedipal motivations. It was better to wait for the transference, Freud counselled.

Another hazard to continuing analyses, was the patient's mistaken belief in his recovery. Termination was to be solely on the initiative of the analyst, Freud warned; alleviation of symptoms was to be avoided; the patient must be kept in a state of "abstinence" (actually he meant "suffering") to keep him anxious for the cure. If the patient felt improved, Freud advised the analyst should then "set up a sufficiently distressing privation again in some other sensitive spot, or else run the risk of never achieving any further improvement except quite insignificant and transitory ones,," One "distressing privation" could be forbidding further relations with a sweetheart; or advising divorce, separation, or other traumatic estrangements.

Freud further advised: If a patient insisted on discontinuing, "I do not conceal from him that no success will result from a treatment broken off after only a small amount of work, and that it may easily like an unfinished operation leave him in an unsatisfactory condition."

In other words the disclaimer of a result in the first interview, somehow did imply a promise of success after all, which would be impossible without continuing patience.

Inch by inch, Freud eliminated all hindrances to his will; the analysis was his possession; he brooked no interference. The analysis must not be discussed outside his chambers. He evaded interference of relatives by accepting only those of independent means. The analysis must become the most important venture of the patient's life; neither career, family or friends must be allowed to interfere. The analysis must be kept going; discontinuances were costly, for then new analysands must be interviewed to replace drop-outs but despite all precautions, unsuitable cases could be accepted. The inference is obvious: Once found amenable, a subject must be kept in psychoanalytic custody indefinitely.

However, one circumstance made it permissible to discontinue analyses — the patient's inability to pay; an unfinished psychic surgery was then unavoidable.

As his cynical directives indicate, Freud became a law unto himself, dictating conditions that relieved analysts of all responsibility while binding his subjects to interminable, expensive psychic contracts. Not only patients but his followers became bent to his spiteful will. Any threat of defection such as Adler, Stekel, Jung and others had perpetrated, reactivated the terror of that eery night when his father growled he would never amount to anything.

When Ernest Jones suggested forming a committee to detect potential defectors, Freud quickly assented. (In his account, Hanns Sachs was not aware the scheme originated with Jones because Freud brought them together to explain it.) Surrounded by Jones, Eitington, Karl Abraham, Rank, Ferenczi and Sachs, Freud instructed them to act as a cohesive, secret group to protect his precious psychoanalysis against rebellion or the over ambitious forming their own schools. Members of the committee were to report to each other secretly, ever on the watch for signs of heresy. In explaining his purpose, Freud used few words, for quoting Sachs,[8] "The purpose for which the association was planned had been discussed between us so often that no long explanation was needed. But we had been quite ignorant of the way in which it could be realized and about that Freud was more explicit."

CHAPTER 6.

# *Conquistador*

*"I am not really a man of science . . . I am nothing but by temperament a conquistador – an adventurer."*

Through the sponsorship of Clark University in 1909, the United States became Freud's first international conquest. No other country in the world has been so lavish in support; in no other country have so many Sigmunds found it so comfortable behind their couches. Yet with characteristic perversity, at no other country did Freud sneer more raucously.

His grudge, originating in an indifference to a digestive upset he suffered here, became tinged with the pathological. Evidently he considered every American an enemy for he bade Hanns Sachs farewell before his departure for America, with:

"Now I know I will have at least one friend in America."

Both G. Stanley Hall and J.J. Putnam, a Boston neurologist, valiant drum beaters for psychoanalysis here only became pariahs for fancied offenses after Freud became recognized.

Freud's conquest here was superbly recorded by Dr. Clarence P. Oberndorf in *A History of Psychoanalysis in America*.[1] Oberndorf was a dissident at heart. Like Ferenczi, he was deeply disappointed with the therapeutic ineffectiveness of Freud's methods. His continued enmeshment can only be accounted for on the basis of a transference he was unable to sever. Despite this transference, Oberndorf retained some critical acumen, colored though it was by his belief in Freud. His ability for honest appraisal is evident throughout his remarkably honest *History of Psychoanalysis in America.*

In including the usual propaganda anent Freud's alienation from the University, Oberndorf represented it as his opportunity to conduct investigations free of restraint. Oberndorf also incorporated Freud's statement to Fliess that his self-analysis had been ameliorative for he felt himself "more normal than I was four or five years ago." The gratifying uplift American recognition had effected, was reflected in Freud's comparison to his European status as an "outcast" whereas in America "I perceived myself accepted by the best men as an equal." Yet, it was not long before Freud became alienated from two of these "best men," G. Stanley Hall and. J. J. Putnam.

The competent reporting in Oberndorf's history of psychoanalysis reflected his early ambition for a journalistic career. With characteristic geniality, Oberndorf recounted that when he told a friend that he had entertained that ambition before studying medicine, his friend exclaimed:

"What are you now? Nothing but a fellow poking around in other people's affairs to satisfy your own curiosity, like any other cheap reporter. Instead of having to chase around town to get your story, you have it brought right to you and get paid for it."

Oberndorf's first reading of Freud's *Three Contributions to the Theory of Infantile Sexuality,* induced neither belief nor a wish to join the movement. That resulted from the recommendations of colleagues. Eventually he became enamoured with the theory but his disappointment with psychoanalytic therapy persisted throughout his career without abating.

In 1950 Oberndorf visited a modern state hospital, with the latest equipment, architecture, lighting and planning. The patients were the same types of the mentally incapacitated he had seen forty years before as an

intern at Manhattan State Hospital. Their histories
revealed some had had protracted psychoanalytic therapy,
as well as interpretations of Rorschach tests, encephelog-
rams, intelligence tests and considerable laboratory work.
In 1910, case histories usually read: "The patient is disinterested, apathetic, sits alone will not work and is deteriorated."

In 1950, "deteriorated" read, "regressed," without any
indication of therapeutic advances, Oberndorf concluded
sadly.

In his private practice, Oberndorf confessed similar
therapeutic stagnation. He attributed some indifference,
even opposition by Freud to achieving therapeutic successes. Brill, Oberndorf's close friend, had proved that
"in some stubborn cases that had been unsuccessfully
treated by prominent physicians with other methods over
many years that psychoanalysis worked well — at times
specifically — in curing a great variety of illnesses."

Brill, however, only felt the hot blasts of Freud's animosity for his therapeutic effectiveness, for when Oberndorf told him that Brill had discarded the couch, the
old monster commented sourly:

"In that too, he is a deviationist."

As the movement heated up, the maneuvering, the
politics, the currying for favor and jockeying for position
intensified. There was a hot line to the throne at Bergasse
19; the conquistador's advice (orders) on every issue was
eagerly sought; he read and passed on every paper submitted for publication. Moreover, as training analyses became
mandatory, Freud could also scrutinize every candidate
through the training analysts' reports to him.

By 1916, psychoanalysis was increasing in popularity.
Training analyses were then instituted as a professional
requisite which of course limited psychoanalytic membership. Training analyses was Jung's suggestion to
eliminate neurotic residues before candidates could enter
practice. Excellent though it was in theory, in practice
it became a bludgeon to indoctrinate Freud's gospel and
crush out independent thought as "resistance."

As was originally true of therapy, the first training analyses were brief, informal affairs. Candidates for a franchise merely arranged for an analysis with a recognized Freudian and his recommendation usually sufficed. As franchises became increasingly lucrative and applicants increased, the time and expense of training analyses also increased, as did the possibilities of rejection.

Already irked by Brill, the independence ot the American disciples further angered Freud. There was some justification in his fear expressed to Hanns Sachs, that he did not have any friends here, for the Americans sometimes flouted his edicts from Vienna. In 1919 Dr. William A. White, superintendent of St. Elizabeth's, the Federal mental hospital and famous for his testimony at the Loeb-Leopold trial, boldly challenged Freud's authority by proclaiming "the time has come to free American psychiatry from the domination of the Pope at Vienna."[2] White demanded the abolishment of the American Psychoanalytic Association and its incorporation with the American Psychopathological Association. Naturally the Freudians fought this; it would have relegated them to an inferior position.

On the other hand, the Pope was jealous of any ties with medicine or any other competing school and advocated that psychoanalysis be a completely separate discipline with its own training facilities. The Americans opposed this too for they were predominantly medically trained physicians and the idea of permitting lay analysts to become their equals was just as repugnant as White's proposal. According to Oberndorf:

"American psychoanalysts never regarded psychoanalysis as a separate discipline but as essentially a branch of psychiatry and medicine. By 1919, psychoanalysis had permeated psychiatric thinking in America to an extent unknown elsewhere."

Freud's couch had become Mecca. In 1919, the first American made his pilgrimage; by 1921, five others including Clarence Oberndorf, followed. At that time, Freud's couch was also warmed by a British devotee and

by Strachey, his translator. Then Freud usually demanded
six seances weekly from patients but relented with professionals for whom only five were mandatory.

Confining himself to professionals gratified Freud in
many ways. His ordainment conferred high status in the
hierarchy and that appealed to his vanity as a "king
maker." His probing would enable him to detect incipient
heresy, always terrifying to his anxiety ridden soul. By
granting audiences to professionals, his influence spread
much wider through the honors he could confer, and the
papers and books he could suggest for publication, all
glorifying his name. Another fear — that his name would
be omitted from their papers as Jung once had — therefore
became allayed. Moreover, as Freud had little interest
in therapy discussing theory, philosophizing, gossiping
and pumping his disciples for information was far more
enjoyable and profitable.

Oberndorf's account of his analysis with Freud is an
invaluable contribution to psychiatry for its detailed
description of how the man worked in the privacy of his
chambers and the hypnotic affects he could induce.

"My own admiration and respect — shall I say awe
of him," Oberndorf recounted, "was very great and it was
with a heart quickened with expectation and anxiety that
I hurried in the twilight down the narrow Bergasse for
my first six o'clock appointment."

The "modesty, almost dinginess" of the little side street
was disappointing. When Freud appeared punctually,
Oberndorf was immediately struck with his deep set brown
eyes, burning with a steady, penetrating, look. "Despite
the general effect of old age (sixty-seven) his movements
were quick and precise, his voice crisp."

Affable in greeting, Freud asked about various American affiliates. After instructing Oberndorf to "lie down
on the couch in the corner; he walked to a chair at its
head, sat down, and to my discomfiture, disappeared from
view. Freud's unceremonious removal of himself proved
definitely disturbing. Possibly I would have preferred to
prolong the short, social conversational contact to study

my man."

Being studied was anathema to Freud; he could not stand "being stared at." The brief look into his burning eyes did much to induce the hypnotic state, as Dr. Oberndorf's passivity discloses, for he obeyed despite his preference for prolonging face to face conversation and study. It was particularly imperative for Freud to deny prolonged observation to a man like Oberndorf, trained to recognize neurotic symptoms.

He was struck by Freud's generally impersonal and detached manner, his uncanny ability for discovering the weak points in a position and pointing them out pitilessly at times. When Freud appeared at the late evening meetings of the Vienna group, after his hours of consultation, according to Oberndorf, he showed little signs of fatigue and "would close the discussion of the papers with penetrating, sometimes caustic words which like a cool blast of air cleared mist. . . . These words were usually authoritative and final . . . the moment his co-workers and students seemed to have been waiting and many a head nodden in assent." His authoritativeness, Oberndorf naively concluded, "gave to Freud's comments an impression of infallibility that he may have had no intention of encouraging."

In their association of five months or about one-hundred seances, Freud remained consistently impersonal though at times he did discuss matters as an equal. His impersonal detachment, Oberndorf concluded with astonishing naivete, may have "acted as a protective armour against his own uncertainties and the unwelcome intrusions of analytic routine into his far more important scientific work and prolific writing."

Considering that Oberndorf had sacrificed five months of practice, had incurred traveling and maintenance expenses as well as Freud's fees, his humility is astounding. Rather than resenting Freud's cool impersonality, he humbly believed that his consultations with him were an unwelcome intrusion upon his "far more important scientific work and prolific writing."

Oberndorf alternated his naivete with some shrewdness, for during his hegira to Vienna he was aware that
the inner circle of the seven rings was operating. "Retro-
spectively," Oberndorf observed, "the idea of a secret
cabinet seems to have been ill-advised. It's purpose to
direct the use of a body of scientific knowledge could,
of course, not be carried out."

As a disciplinary body enforcing the psychoanalytic
line, it was enormously effective in Europe but less in
the United States where Brill was regarded as the leader.
There is every reason to believe that Freud resented Brill's
independence and was anxious to unseat him. Oberndorf
suspected that H. W. Frink whose analysis with Freud
was concurrent with his own, may have become designated
as the leader of the American branch, or at least of the
New York society. Each of several other pilgrims in the
1921 group may also have felt they had been chosen by
Freud because violent dissension broke out among them.
As a consequence, Oberndorf reported that several prospective psychoanalysts became so repelled by the bitter
feuding they lost interest and withdrew.

Oberndorf's suspicion that Frink was groomed to oust
Brill was aroused by his scathing review of Brill's book
on basic psychoanalysis which Brill's friends furiously
resented. Dissension flared; Frink then suffered a nervous
breakdown from which he never completely recovered.
American psychoanalysis lost a gifted, devoted disciple,
Oberndorf sadly observed for several years later, Frink
died, still comparatively young.

Oberndorf could be regarded as ambivalent, both en-
tranced and repelled by Freud who advocated completely
inconsistent principles. Though contending sexual repression caused neuroses, he advised sexual abstinence to
bring out "latent anxiety." Although supposedly opposed
to active therapy, Oberndorf learned from associates that
Freud once sent a man who feared the dead to visit a
cemetery in darkest night. He was also known to actively
and caustically criticize analysands for lack of cooperation
and for their behavior away from his couch.

During these postwar troubled times, Vienna mobs rioted over lack of fuel and food, Freud became pale and nervous when he heard about it, so after his seance, Oberndorf frequented some of the neighborhood taverns to investigate the rioting. Almost unanimously, the Viennese condemned the "damned" Americans and Wilson's fourteen points. When Oberndorf mentioned his tour of inquiry in his next seance, Freud asked with alarmed astonishment:

"You went out alone?"

In summarizing his one hundred hours on the Couch of Couches, Oberndorf was less than enthusiatic and rationalized that his absence from the anxieties and problems of his environment while living in a holiday atmosphere, detracted from the value of his analysis with Freud, though he believed somewhat vaguely that his insight had improved. He could not decide whether or not increasing his course to two or three hundred hours would have augmented its benefits.

In their last seance, with a cool, impersonal handshake, Freud made this astonishing summary of the analysis:

"We harbor no hard feelings."

Evidently he believed that if his animosity was not aroused, that was a sufficient accomplishment. However, hard feelings did erupt because of Oberndorf's efforts to exclude lay analysts from the American societies which were bitterly opposed by Freud and his European disciples. In 1929 Brill visited Freud who was forced to accept this compromise: If the Europeans would agree not to accept trainees unless cleared by the American Education Committee (from which Oberndorf immediately resigned as head) the New Yorkers would in turn agree to accept lay members.

The New Yorkers then neatly double crossed the Europeans by stipulating that lay trainees must spend a year in a psychiatric hospital. They could just as well have stipulated that they spend a year on the moon, for psychiatric hospitals did not accept laymen except as orderlies. Medical qualifications for full membership were later restored, to complete the double cross.

In the crazy world of psychoanalysis, it all worked to Freud's advantage for psychoanalysis attained dizzier and dizzier heights because of its medical affiliation and virtually dominated psychiatry for the next several decades. Had Freud won his fight for lay analysis, he would have lost status as a scientist and become merely another leader of a cult, as he was always regarded in Europe.

Unaware that he had actually been fortunate in losing to the Americans when Oberndorf visited Freud last in 1929, he growled:

"What have you really got against lay analysis?"

That Oberndorf became disenchanted with the analytical method can be confirmed from his subsequent approach. He decried the use of the couch, worked face to face and reviewed Freud's later publications with growing skepticism. His *Ego and Id*, was as compartmented as a department store, Oberndorf criticized. According to Wittels, Freud had written *Totem and Taboo* to compete with Jung's treatise on folk psychology. Similarly, Oberndorf believed that *Inhibition, Symptom and Anxiety* was motivated against Wilhelm Reich.

As psychoanalytic therapy deteriorated in effectiveness, Oberndorf became increasingly disenchanted. He endorsed a fellow practitioner's wistful hope that he could once more secure his excellent results "before knowing so much psychoanalysis." Oberndorf's increasing concern may have come from realizing that psychoanalysis was primarily Sigmund Freud's successful self-promotion. In his last interview with the seer he was astonished by Freud's intimate acquaintance with his most active American followers and his detailed information about how papers were discussed and by whom.

Oberndorf's suspicion that Freud had instigated Frink's attack upon Brill would therefore appear justified in view of his close surveillance of the American scene. It would also justify a suspicion that Freud also simultaneously planted the same ambition in the eager minds of other Americans then on his couch to select the victor from the consequent infighting.*

Eventually Oberndorf completely renounced and abandoned the orthodox Freudian therapy. He found that five or six seances per week were superfluous; that analyses could be interrupted without harm to the patient; that dreams were not the "royal road" to the unconscious and varied with the whims o the interpreter. He also concluded that training analyses subjected trainees to rigorous, stereotyped thinking and indelibly stamped the trainer's ideas upon his pupil after their prolonged intimacy.

Oberndorf decried the lack of any "classical" studies of consecutive psychoanalytic cases followed for five years. In 1952, members of the American Psychoanalytic Association resisted his proposal that such results be compiled even on their own definition of healing. Only about one half of his colleagues answered his questionnaires; few would reveal their results or agree to send patients who had been in their care for a year before a panel to examine the advisability of further Freudo-analysis.

In his quest for a definition of psychoanalysis, Oberndorf cited Freud's cryptic summary that it was "the study of processes of which we are unaware of what for the sake of brevity we call the unconscious, by the free association technique of analyzing observable phenomena of transference and resistance."

It is significant that Freud did not claim therapy was incorporated in the method and attended this so-called "study."

Oberndorf's proposals must have been a thorn to the orthodox Freudians but they never risked a fight with him. His integrity and his thorough knowledge of Freudian politics and chicanery would have made him a dangerous antagonist. He was left alone; the wily Freudians paid lip service to his eminence but evaded all his suggestions and proposals. He was too dangerous to attack as an heretic and died without incurring that label.

*As will be disclosed in the next chapter, Freud eventually found his ideal leader in Franz Alexander.

## CHAPTER 7

# American Fuehrer

*"You see I have amounted to something after all."*

In Franz Alexander, Freud found the ideal director of his movement in the United States. This short, compactly built man was colorful and flamboyant with the pugnacity of a bulldog. Alexander was the first student enrolled at the Berlin Institute of Psychoanalysis in 1920, and soon after his graduation came to Freud's notice. He settled in the United States in 1930 but returned to visit Freud three times, the last in 1935.

Alexander's obituary on Freud, "Memories of Bergasse 19,"[1] corroborates Oberndorf in respect to Freud's avid interest in his disciples: a call upon him was considered obligatory for those visiting Vienna. Freud complained to Alexander of one "important" analyst who had never climbed the Bergasse for a chat and muttered something about "ambivalence." According to Alexander, this anonymous personality who had made "important contributions," eventually became hostile.

Such vagueness is typically Freudian. Why the anonymous analyst was ambivalent; whether his hostility was published, verbal or otherwise manifested, is unexplained. Freud seldom mentioned his critics by name nor quoted any criticisms verbatim. His followers ape him in this respect, as in so many others.

Alexander's hypnotic subjection can be judged from his

avowal that on his first visit to Freud, he was "fully aware
I was facing one of the greatest minds of all time . . .
The shadow of centuries fell over his study and one felt
that one was facing an intellectual mountain peak of
which only a few in each age are connected with each
other by invisible ranges."

The Great One was of course extremely broad of outlook, according to Alexander, he would consider "suggestions not corresponding with his, (but) I must say my
contributions were along the lines he initiated."

Alexander's idolatry is loaded with such double think.
He was apparently oblivious to Freud's tendency to duck
any therapeutic responsibility. Though Freud acknowledged being "aware of the limitations of his therapy, due
to the rigidity and weakness of human character," his
own culpability in devising so rigid a technique is ignored.

Again: True, Alexander explained, Freud could be
impatient and intolerant, but "only when intellectual
integrity was involved." As the record shows, this lack
of integrity in others became most obvious when his sexuality was questioned. As for the healing mechanism, Alexander professed no surprise when Freud said "success was
based on faith in the analyst even though the patient
may never see him again." This faith must be maintained
permanently because the "egos of most people are too
weak."

Since people needed a faith, psychoanalysis supplied
it; Freud told Alexander as much by stating that as
orthodox religious faith weakened with the march of science, robbing man "of a heavenly God, he would tend
to worship small caliber human Gods."

Freud also both acknowledged and alibied for his
"ritualistic" technique which he defended as not being
as rigid and orthodox as most others. He considered his
ritualism was necessary because individualized
techniques would demand an "independent judgment
beyond most physicians." Not only were patients then
too weak to endure a flexible technique but physicians
(meaning of course analysts) were incompetent to use it.

Franz Alexander's indoctrination, in view of his forceful temperament, is unbelievable. It is more believable that he followed the line and paid obeisance to Freud because it paid off handsomely for his was one of the most spectacular careers in the movement. Soon after Freud's passing he showed his skepticism by boldly advocating drastic and heretical changes in technique[2] impossible when Freud was living.

In 1956, Franz Alexander resigned as director of the Chicago Institute and left for the happiest of Freudian hunting grounds, balmy Los Angeles with its zany movie personnel clamoring for encouchment. In farewell, the *Chicago Magazine* (October 1956) published "Franz Alexander, the Man Who Brought Freud Here," in the form of an interview with his daughter which delineates his spectacular career.

Alexander's Budapest background was highly respectable. His father was a professor and editor of the Hungarian *Journal of Philosophy*. After serving for four years in World War I as a medical officer, Alexander worked in the laboratory of a neuropsychiatric institute as a physiologist. When a schizophrenic constantly "pestered" him with his dreams, he recalled reading Freud's *The Interpretation of Dreams* which he confessed he thought was "crazy" at the time.

Thinking "the crazy book might help me to understand the crazy patient," Alexander succumbed himself to Freud's irrationality and abandoned his physiological and medical career for psychoanalysis. He confessed that his decision was "difficult" as the "new science" (one of his favorite expressions) conflicted with his previous training, but he goaded himself on with this bit of weird thinking:

"I found that here after all, was an intellectual edifice which had some familiarity and appeal — it reminded me somewhat of the structure of theoretical physics."

The how and where of this resemblance, Alexander deigned not to clarify. Had Alexander ever paused to consider that a schizophrenic's intense interest in dreams could also indicate schizophrenia in the author of a

dreamology, the "new science" may not have been as allur-
ing.

But attracted he was. Freud chose well for Alexander
was tough, uncompromising and shrewd. His real reasons
for embracing Freud's craft could have been quite different
from those he professed. For so flamboyant a personality
to spend his life in dull laboratory work for which he,
like Freud, may not have had any real gift or inclination
would have been catastrophic. Freud, too, had abandoned
physiology and neurology for the glamor of dream
interpretation. Also like him, Alexander had a natural
gift of gab, or at least a gift for hiring competent ghost
writers, for it is difficult to believe he mastered English
sufficiently well to publish so many articles and books
of his own composition.

In 1930 Alexander was invited to deliver a paper at
the Mental Health Congress in Washington and attracted
the favorable notice of Hutchins, president of the University of Chicago who offered him the post of Visiting Professor of Psychiatry for one year. When Alexander boldly
demanded he be designated "Professor of Psychoanalysis"
he was so ordained.

Proceeding cautiously, for so he confessed, Alexander's
first lecture to the medical caculty was on the work of
Charcot, Bernheim and Lieubeault in hypnosis which
"proved the existence of unconscious processes." This is
the oft repeated insinuation that psychoanalysis is a logical development from hypnosis, whereas it is only a perversion of hypnosis.

Trouble immediately arose in his first lecture, for
someone whom Alexander characteristically refrained
from identifying asked if psychoanalysis was based on
controlled laboratory experiments. The questioner could
very well have been Professor C. Judson Herrick, author
of *The Brains of Rats and Men,* renowned both for his
work in neurological physiology and his aversion for the
"new science."

When Coyne Campbell* told Professor Herrick, his
teacher, that he planned to become an analyst, his disgust

*Coyne Campbell, M.D., (1903-1957), author of Induced Delusions, (Regent House,
1957). See pages 104-105 for details.

was so intense he turned on his heel and walked away
without a word. When Alexander replied to his questioner
that controlled laboratory experiments were not incorporated into Freudian procedures, but requested waiting
until he could outline their method of investigation, the
questioner and several companions quickly rose and left.

Alexander immediately used his hot line to Vienna
to report the incident to Freud, who "was incensed over
the philosophical naivete which prevailed among medical
men, both here and in Europe. He wrote back suggesting
that I ask the seminar participants whether they
regarded astronomy or paleontology as exact sciences —
neither are based on experiment; man cannot bring the
stars into the laboratory and a fossil will not tell him
much when he has done so."

An overwhelming evidence indicates that astronomy
at least, if not also paleontology, is an exact science, based
on the exact sciences of mathematics, physics and chemistry. Astronomy also utilizes the most sophisticated
cameras, telescopes, spectroscopes and other precision
instruments, and thus actually does bring the stars into
the laboratory. Alexander fails to mention whether or
not he confronted the dissenting seminar participants
with Freud's specious argument, but he did go on to incor-
porate his lectures into *The Medical Value of
Psychoanalysis*,[3] a book designed to induce the medical
profession to refer patients for psychoanalysis. The tome
is primarily a theoretical discourse, conveying the impression theory has been confirmed in practice and research.
Detailed case histories are not presented; only two actual
cases are mentioned, but too briefly to be of value.

In identifying Freud's research instrument, Alexander
boldly asserted: "Psychology as an empirical science of
personality began with the discovery of free association."
Note that it is psychology, not psychoanalysis, which owes
its empirical beginnings to free association. Then, possibly
frightened by his audacity, Alexander soft-pedalled: "This
simple procedure seems at first to be a rather trivial device
and it is not so easy to appreciate its value in research,

but is no less true that the methods of percussion and
ausculation appear unpretentious and trivial, and it is
only the interpretation of the small acoustic deviations
that make them so important for medicine."

However, the skeptical streak that Alexander was to
display in later years, cropped out when he took up the
delicate matter of hypnotism:

"It is hard to reconstruct precisely all the motives
which induced him (Freud) to give up hypnotic treatments
and I do not think that even he is able fully to account
for it. The reasons stated in his writings do not appear
entirely satisfactory."

Like a patient on the couch who is allowed to flit to
another free association because his last was too dangerous to explore, Alexander drifted off to depreciate the value
of recalling traumatic experiences through hypnotism
because they lacked "pathogenic significance."

It was not entirely scientific investigaion however,
that had confirmed the verity of psychoanalysis; Alexander hailed as corroborators, the "great *menschenkenner*"
of authors, novelists and dramatists. "Only these have
been able to overcome to some degree most of the difficulties in understanding people's real motives in spite
of the human tendency to deceive oneself as well as
others," he asserted.

Who these authors of so much insight were and their
masterpieces, Alexander omitted mentioning. In that he
imitated Freud who constantly made similarly gran-
diloquent but also vague assertions, as if their truth was
so obvious proof was superfluous. Freud's method was also
portrayed as unique; far superior to other methods, for
he had created, Alexander pontificated, "a reasoned and
exact psychological method in contrast to all other
methods, successful or not, based much more on vague
empirical observations than through understanding the
therapeutic process itself." More:

"An insight into fundamental psychodynamic structure is the principle contribution of psychoanalysis to
psychiatry." Another gem:

"The first woman, Eve, seduced Adam by giving him the apple which is a symbolic reference to the female breasts."

To illustrate Freudian understanding of the therapeutic process, Alexander triumphantly presented a cure he had worked himself. His patient was a young unhappy bride, severely constipated. Upon learning her husband neglected shows of affection, Alexander called in the man, an egocentric artist, and suggested he show his love by bringing home flowers to his languishing bride.

After the artist "said it with flowers," his wife dramatically responded with "a spontaneous bowel movement," her first in two years without resorting to an enema, and the cure persisted for five years, to the glory of psychoanalysis. Unfortunately Alexander failed to mention the use of free association, dream interpretation or any other Freudian device to prove his cure was effected thereby. In fact, the omission of pure psychoanalytic cures could indicate no such cases existed, or that Alexander feared such presentations would appear ridiculous to the medical profession.

As Jung discovered through Krafft-Ebing, the psychiatrist demonstrates his own subjective leanings through the material he selects for elaboration. Alexander's subjection was displayed in dwelling upon Freud's martyrdom, for he waxed highly emotional, and considered it "tactless to guess at Freud's subjective reasons for wishing his own creation to remain separate from medicine if his motives did not have so profoundly human a justification. There is no question that Freud deeply resents the refusal of medicine to appreciate his life work."

Alexander himself may therefore also have suffered some indignities from the medical establishment which led to his psychoanalytic affiliation. He attributed Freud's bitterness to the "laughter" he received upon reporting his work with Charcot, which "will remain always a classical example of the dogmatic attitude of medicine toward its great representatives and reminds one of the reception of Harvey's Pasteur's and Semmelweiss'," Alexander indignantly concluded.

At the time he was greeted with "laughter," Freud had just started practice. True, he met with some ridicule and skepticism, but his own abrasive offensiveness and his tendency to magnify slights must be considered. There may also really have been some jealousy and bigotry involved because of the medical rivalry of Vienna and Paris, but on the main, Freud's discourse was received civilly. The "laughter" was not intended entirely for Freud; it was directed primarily toward Charcot who was something of a showman and poseur. Charcot's ideas on hysteria and hypnotism that Freud presented were disputed by Bernheim, now regarded as a far more competent authority on hypnotism than Charcot whose concepts never attained permanent status.

These are some of the facts about Freud's reception that have been distorted and exaggerated as the same form of fiendish injustice that Harvey, Semmelweiss and Pasteur suffered. It is clever propaganda, and amazingly effective. Alexander closed his arguments with a similar ploy now also standard propaganda: Psychiatry has incorporated Freud without accrediting him and now uses his ideas "with slight changes in terminology."

Just what these stolen inspirations were, what they accomplish and who are the thieves, are not mentioned. Oberndorf did cite one example of such borrowing: The patients diagnosed as "deteriorated" in the psychiatric case histories of 1910, became described as "regressed" in 1950 without improvement in either case.

Publication of Alexander's brief touched off a fierce controversy in the pages of the *American Journal of Psychiatry*. Dr. Bernard Sachs, well known for his opposition, reviewed the book as "The False Claims of the Psychoanalysts" in the January 1933 issue, "to enter a protest against tht uncritical adoption of many questionable theories and to put medical men, neurologists and psychiatrists on their guard."

Doctor Sachs objected to the Freudian exaggerations of the dominance of the unconscious mind over the powers of reasoning inherent in conscious thinking. Had he known then of Freud's disavowal of unconscious phenomena of 1897, he could have accused Alexander of trying to sell a dead horse.

Doctor Sachs also decried the sorry cases coming to him for treatment after years on the couch, burdened by the morbid suggestions of incest, parricidal lusts and latent homosexuality. "Nowadays a true Freudian denies any suggestion of hypnotic influence" he charged, "and is wholly devoted to 'free association,'" which Doctor Sachs contended inevitably takes a desultory course, leading nowhere and prolonging treatment to intolerable lengths.

Franz Alexander's rejoinder, published as "A Voice from the Past," repeated the old propaganda that objections to Freud were based on the same ignorance which condemned Harvey et al., and that psychoanalysis was already incorporated into psychiatry. He indignantly objected to Sachs' derogation of his colleagues as "infantilists" and nobly disavowed any intention to follow Sachs "in this violent tone . . . the powerless anger of an exponent of a lost cause . . . Modern psychiatry . . . has to a large extent accepted psychoanalytic concepts. It is no exaggeration that psychoanalysis has become fundamental to modern psychopathology."

As usual, a specific mention of a Freudian idea used in psychiatry is avoided. Also as was his practice, Alexander dutifully reported the Sachs review to Freud, who replied with his usual acrimony, that "the only thing true in it," was that he and Sachs had once been classmates. Yet Sachs had charged no more than Freud himself admitted in his communications to Fliess and Alexander was to admit in 1946 in his heretic *"Psychoanalytic Therapy."*

Alexander rose to fame as director of the Chicago Institute. He was a tough, pugnacious individual whom Coyne Campbell knew well and had seen him almost come to blows with Zilboorg, analyzer of Marshall Field III. Franz Alexander accused Zilboorg of hypnotizing Field.

He also accused Zilboorg of exploiting Field's feelings of guilt for the huge inheritance from his ruthless grandfather whose memory he tried to erase by re-naming the Marshall Field Museum simply the Field Museum.

Alexander's real reason for his anger may have been envy of Zilboorg's huge fee, reputedly the largest ever paid for a psychoanalysis. Regardless of how much he paid, on the couch Marshall Field III was only grist for the Freudian mill. The standard interpretations were delivered under hypnotic influences, as Alexander's accusation certainly indicated.

In 1946 the irrepressible Alexander made these serious admissions in the introduction to his *Psychoanalytic Therapy*:[3]

"Like most psychoanalysts, we have been puzzled by the unpredictability of therapeutic results, by the baffling discrepancy between the length and intensity of treatment and the degree of therapeutic success. It is not unusual for a patient to get well as the result of a few consultations; for even a severe neurotic condition with psychotic elements to yield to brief therapeutic work. Yet another case which seems comparatively mild may not respond to a systematic treatment of many years. That there is no simple correlation between therapeutic results and the length and intensity of treatment has been recognized, tacitly or explicitly, by most experienced psychoanalysts and is an old source of dissatisfaction among them."

Confessing his inability to differentiate between a seemingly mild case and a severe one would appear to substantiate the charge of Doctor Sachs in 1933 that the Freudians had no reliable criteria for diagnosis and treatment. If true, a seemingly mild case that does not "respond for years," could have become severe because Freudian treatment only aggravated the illness. Severe cases "with psychotic elements" discharged after brief treatments, may have been dismissed prematurely. The possibilities of error are boundless.

Undertones of sarcasm and contempt underlie Alexander's criticisms of his colleagues for their failures and complacency, which he alleged was a "self deceptive defense in the form of an almost superstitious belief that quick therapeutic results cannot be genuine, that they are either those transitory results due to suggestion or an escape into 'pseudo-health' by patients who prefer to give up their symptoms rather than obtain real insight."

Despite quick results which have become permanent (his case of the unhappy bride's resolution of her unhappiness and constipation when her husband "said it with flowers," would seem apropos) orthodox Freudians continue to argue against quick improvements because they insist that years are needed to effect fundamental personality changes. Others, Alexander charged, blame prolonged analyses on "resistance," and "comfort themselves by saying the patient is not yet 'fully analyzed' and continued treatment will eventually succeed." When they fail instead, they diagnose the patient as a "latent schizophrenic."

"We shall not attempt to refute all the unwritten superstitions in our field. Every science has prejudices concerning its unexplored territories," he morosely concluded.

It was a magnificent show of integrity but unfortunately Alexander did not accuse the real culprit, Sigmund Freud, who had so indelibly planted the very ideas Alexander deplored. Every prejudice and superstition Alexander fumed against was reiterated in Freud's "Analysis, Terminable and Interminable,"[4] and every attempt to improve technique had met his furious opposition.

Had Alexander pondered Freud aversion for therapy he may have begun to question the soundness of his own judgment in adopting psychoanalysis as a career after his attempt to understand the "crazy" through a book he had initially also thought "crazy."

Admitting error was probably just as horrifying to Alexander as it was for Freud. He did this indirectly by advocating abandoning the free association technique (which he had so blatantly heralded as brilliant scientific discovery) for direct questioning. He also derided the transference as a worthless healing instrument, and condemned permitting uninhibited behavior and talk by patients and advocated reducing the frequency and duration of treatment. Essentially Alexander called for a new deal in psychoanalysis, contradicting all that was heretofore considered holy Freud, as Ferenczi, Stekel, Adler, Oberndorf and other dissidents had, only to encounter the Master's hatred and invective.

Alexander's daring innovations met no more cooperation than had Oberndorf's. Still, the Freudian boom kept soaring; Los Angeles became the Freudian capitol and Alexander governed there as director of the psychiatric clinic at the huge Mount Sinai-Cedars of Lebanon complex. He conducted training analyses which ran about 400 hours, quite modest considering 1000-1500 hours are now being logged. When Alexander died in 1964, psychoanalysis was at its zenith; it had virtually taken over psychiatry.

In his opening paragraph to "Psychiatry Here and in England," the British psychiatrist William Sargant wrote:[5]

"Most psychiatrists visiting the United States from abroad are bewildered at the way the direction and control of American psychiatry have been taken over since World War II by psychoanalysts who are ideological followers of Freud and now sometimes call themselves 'dynamically orientated' psychiatrists."

Dr. Sargant went on to describe various advances in psychiatric treatment such as group psychotherapy of alcoholism in a religious setting; administering penicillin for general paralysis of the insane; and vitamin $B_2$ (nicotinic acid), for pellagrous madness and neuroses once so common in our South; simple thyroid extract in the neuroses and for the madness common to myxedema; epileptic manifestations yielding to simple drug treatment and neurosurgical techniques; electroshock in severe and intractable melancholia which formerly doomed many to die after years in mental institutions; leucotomy (lobotomy); tranquilizers effective in acute and chronic schizophrenia; antidepressant drugs relieving anxiety states. Dr. Sargant summarized:

"In fact, apart from senility, mental defects, adolescent psychopathy, sexual deviations, few mild or serious mental illnesses are now without some means of help by increasingly simple biological and chemical treatments."

According to Doctor Sargant, these treatments are proving very effective in England and other countries free of Freudian domination. In the United States such methods are ignored and neglected. Sargant attributed our sad decline in psychiatric treatment to the awesome power of the Freudians which enables them to discredit all other methods. Sargant also contended the Freudians have made it "increasingly difficult to obtain any high academic or university teaching post in general psychiatry, especially in a general medical school unless one has made a personal training analysis, Freudian style, with complete conversion to the ideology."

Breast frustration in infancy is diagnosed *a là Freud* as the cause of depression, despite the success of biochemical methods Sargant mentioned. Once totally committed to their ideology, the Freudians become increasingly afraid "of allowing any other methods of psychiatric treatment to gain any real recognition and acceptance in medical schools and teaching centers."

Sargant is highly qualified on discussing conversion for his work *The Battle for the Mind*,[6] is a classic on the subject. Candidates for a Freudian franchise are subjected to the same "we guaratee nothing" proposition as patients. According to Sargant: "The anxiety situation certainly helps some to speed up their 'conversion' in order to start earning a living. He must accept the ideology or risk rejection and the waste of his time and money."

A Freudian convert directed our National Institute of Mental Health Dr. Sargant indicated, the Institute's number two man was also once encouched. He also stated that Freudians advise the Ford and Rockefeller Foundations on their grants which they steer to Freudian oriented institutions. Journals of great influence in psychiatry, Dr. Sargant also noted, were then under Freudian thumbs, and only a few non-Freudians had top posts in psychiatric teaching because submitting to analysis has become a requisite. Schools in the South and Mid-West who had resisted the Freudian infiltration found it increasingly difficult to secure grants.

Through analysis (really hypnotism) the Freudians control key figures in teaching centers, editorial posts, hospitals and institutions. Power is everything, as Freud so shrewdly knew. As conqueror of psychiatry, he made his own laws and possible for his followers to do as they damn pleased. How it pleases them, can be gleaned from this reminiscence of Dr. Sargant when he told some "former psychoanalytic friends and colleagues at the Massachusetts General Hospital" of his fine results in treating battle neuroses, shell shock and other war incurred psychiatric disorders.

"We hear your group did supposedly great things in the war," said a Freudian patronizingly, "but they really don't amount to anything, since you cannot explain how your treatments worked."

Unfortunately Doctor Sargant did not or could not tell him that freudo-analysis works by inducing a form of hypnotism to keep a subject bound to the couch interminably until he succumbs to their insinuations that he suffers from a suppressed passion to cohabit with his mother and kill his father as a love rival, a la Sigmund Freud.

## CHAPTER 8

# The Decline

*"All psychology is psychoanalysis."*

In the fifties, even as the Freudians were attaining
the domination described by Sargant, countervailing
influences started working. In 1954, there was published
*Fragments of an Analysis with Freud,* a first hand account
of four months on his couch in 1934 by Joseph Wortis.[1]
As a description of how Freud worked in the privacy of
his chambers it is invaluable, considering that he formed
his conclusions from purely verbal, unwitnessed and
unrecorded transactions. His interpretations there-
forecould not be checked against any data. A patient's
objections to his interpretations were dismissed as "resistance." Imagine Freud's reaction if a patient questioned
his Oedipal diagnostics!

Wortis, however, was not the typical patient for his
was a didactic analysis sponsored by a financial backer
he declined to reveal. He was also coached from behind
the scenes by Havelock Ellis and Dr. Adolph Meyer which
gave his transaction an air of espionage. It is doubtful
that Freud ever undertook analysis under such conditions or with such an incumbent of his couch for Wortis
possessed such self-confidence and aplomb, he man-
ipulated Freud with remarkable ease. Immediately after
each seance he recorded his notes on 4x6 cards which
now constitute a transcript that is the most complete and

authentic on record of seances with Freud.

Wortis was advised by Havelock Ellis: "It would be better to follow his *example* rather than his precept. He did not begin by being psychoanalyzed (never was) or attaching himself to any sect or school, but went about freely, studying the work of others and retaining always his own independence." In following that advice, Wortis not only escaped Freud's domination, an astonishing feat in itself, but actually achieved a mastery over him. Completely unawed, he became a case of strong *Widerstand* (resistance) without developing a transference and continually baffled the seer of Vienna with his clever change of pace and switch of subjects.

Wortis was very adroit at cooling Freud's anger with ingratiating references to his fame and renown whenever he got into hot water. That was often, for the sessions were punctuated with constant bickering. Dissension began immediately after appointments were scheduled and the fees set, for then Wortis had the effrontery to stipulate his agreement with Freud, was subject to final approval by his financial sponsor. If approval were withheld, only completed sessions would then be paid for, he hedged.

Freud took umbrage at this and rebuked Wortis for involving him in a cancellable contract. Nevertheless, he started the analysis with this humiliating reservation but insisted that Wortis immediately cable his sponsor for approval. Ever the business man, Freud evidently could not bear losing a fee of $1600 for the four months, or approximately eighty seances involved. It is also quite possible that Wortis sensed his anxiety for the fee and delighted in toying with him.

Challenging any of his opinions irritated Freud; he labeled Wortis' independence *Widerstand*. Speaking too low, was also *Widerstand*. (Freud would not admit his impaired hearing; he was seventy-eight at the time.) When Wortis was tardy (which was often) that too was *Widerstand*. Before long, *Widerstand* dominated the interpretations. Yet with incredible aplomb, Wortis succeeded in diverting Freud to topics he wished discussed; into provoking many significant admissions from him, into berating his enemies and spouting off on a wide variety of topics. Divining the old boy was quite susceptible to flattery, Wortis laid it on thick. Wortis also sensed his innate perversity and confessed that he felt "the surest way to coax him to say something was to say the opposite."

Once when reprimanded for *Widerstand,* Wortis saucily replied:

"You act as if psychoanalysis stood high and perfect and only our own faults keep us from accepting it; it does not seem to occur to you that it is simply polite to reckon with one's own prejudices."

"Analysis is not a place for polite exchanges," Freud answered coldly. "I observed that you had a certain amount of *Widerstand* and set about to remove it," thus betraying that he could use an active technique when his ego was ruffled.

Freud spoke in a lecture platform style, Wortis observed, and repeated much well known, published material. This could indicate that his assertion that psychoanalysis could only be learned on the couch, was another misrepresentation for in his seances he merely reiterated long familiar notions available in print.

Wortis often chatted about the lectures he attended, the books he read, his letters from Havelock Ellis, and commented on ideas and people Freud detested. These hints that the analysis was not center stage could also have jarred Freud's vanity. He accused Wortis of dodging unpleasant truths, his stock charge against critics, dissenters and society in general. When Freud scornfully ridiculed his talents for psychology, Wortis replied with a mixture of insolence and flattery:

"That is too bad since I shall probably continue my work in psychology anyway. I consider you the greatest

psychologist we have had and I hould have liked nothing
better than a word of encouragement. I'm sorry I have
got just the opposite."

"There is no need to show you any consideration,"
Freud shrewdly countered, "you have a degree of self-
confidence that fortifies you against criticism. It is really
enviable."

Freud exploded at mention of Stekel whom he accused
of pettiness, overambition, treachery and venality. When
Wortis tried to placate him with the assurance that Stekel
still greatly admired him, Freud scoffed: "It's only a pose."
He kept fuming about Stekel's offenses which included
making point blank interpretations of Oedipal motivations without waiting for the transference. The transference, Freud said, was no longer a mechanism of cure but
a means to bring "unconscious material to consciousness."
But baring unconscious motivations was always represented as the mechanism of cure, and if the transference
worked to that effect, it was still curative.

What Freud may have felt, unconsciously of course,
was that transference as an emotional relationship
between patient and analyst was too much of a strain.
Using the transference to bare the unconscious, or to put
it another way, to regress the patient as in hypnotism,
and keep him regressed by withholding the suggestions
which would awake him from his regressive state, keeps
the patient in a state of transference without involving
the analyst emotionally.

Wortis' clever needling provoked Freud into expressing his opinions on everything from Adler to Zionism,
on his detractors, his disciples, on homosexuality, money,
Einstein, character and talent. Of his opinions, there was
no end. They flowed as copiously as free associations; as
undirected, uncensored and irrelevant as babblings from
his couch. A few samples:

"People are not honest, they don't admit their ignorance and that is why they write such nonsense; a father
who raises his son without a mother will make a homosex-

ual of him; children mistrust their parents because of sex lies told them; dreaming of going to the theatre always means coitus; all psychology is psychoanalysis, what is left is the physiology of the senses."

Wortis also reveals this amusing instance of Freud's capricious memory, which he relied upon as a scientific recording instrument: Freud had mentioned that Havelock Ellis had complained in a letter to him that Ernest Jones had written an unfavorable review of one of his books. When Ellis was informed, he replied to Wortis in astonishment that the review was in Jones' "most superior and supercilious tone," and he had never read further after one glance, nor had written to Freud about it. Mrs. Ellis, however, had written to Freud to erase the impression fostered by Jones that Ellis was hostile to him.

"This was the supposed 'protest' by me!" Havelock Ellis informed Wortis. "It would, of course, anyhow been absurd to send a protest to one man against a criticism written by another."

True, Freud was almost senile at the time and suffering from a painful cancer, but the same inadequacies were apparent in his prime. As a youth, he was often querulous, constantly bickering, complaining and imputing the lowest of motives to others. Wortis' account, despite his questionable motives and methods, jibes with many other reports of Freud's seances. If an eavesdropper were to publish Freud's dialogue with a patient, it would not be as valuable as the Wortis diary because he was a participant and included his own reactions as well as his technique for inciting Freud's self-exposure.

Another exposure contributing to the decline was Emil Ludwig's *Doctor Freud*[2]. His interview with Freud in 1927, seven years before Wortis and six years after Oberndorf, corroborates their accounts in many details. Ludwig, however, was a skeptic free of awe, immune to Freud's hypnotic powers who conversed with him face to face as an equal.

Even before they met, Ludwig confessed he had been impressed by the "deep-set, dark scrutinizing eyes" in his portrait and by his courteous consent to an interview in

a "lively, polite note in his own handwriting." When he
called, Ludwig was further impressed by the simplicity
of his residence, his "unadorned appearance (and) the ear-
nestness of his glance, which at close range seemed less
penetrating than meditative." At the time, Freud was
seventy and bore the pain of his cancer with a courage
and dignity Ludwig commended.

As they conversed, however, Ludwig soon became
aware of a cold impersonality and a rigid outlook. They
differed over Goethe and da Vinci, subjects of two Ludwig
biographies, but clashed most violently over Napoleon.
When Freud asked in "his pedagogic tone," who was
Napoleon's favorite brother, Ludwig answered, "Lucien,"
Freud then contradicted, "No . . . Joseph."

According to Ludwig, Napoleon was fondest of his
youngest brother and treated him like a son. He tried
to make a king of Lucien and arranged a royal marriage,
but succeeded only in rendering him unhappy. Eventually
Lucien renounced his throne, married the girl he loved
and went off to write a novel, his most cherished desire.

"When I saw that he was ignorant of Napoleon's relations with his brothers, but required Joseph," Ludwig
wrote, "So I merely said, 'Just as you please; Joseph. And
what about him?' "

Napoleon saw Joseph as a father substitute, Freud
interpreted, and discoursed at length upon Joseph's influence, concluding:

"Because he felt *Joseph* to be his father, Napoleon
married a woman called *Josephine*. And in recollection
of Joseph, he went off to Egypt." This was of course his
incestual obsession, now applied to Joseph with a
homosexual tinge, for Napoleon's attraction to Josephine
was interpreted as a displacement for his latent homosexuality. Unaware of Freud's incest-homosexual obsessions,
Ludwig was astonished by his puerility in basing it on
a similarity in names.

"I thought I was dreaming," Ludwig confessed, "but
as that would have been dangerous in Freud's presence,
I pulled myself together and received the second fantasy

with a nod."

Depressed over these puerilities, Ludwig walked all
the way back to his hotel, eager for fresh air, as if he
had just "emerged from a cave." Freud's interpretations
of three figures "well known to me (Goethe, da Vinci and
Napoleon) seem musty caricatures . . . His revelations
had chilled me particularly because they were put forward
in a calm and cold voice with indomitable seriousness.
I knew nothing of their having been printed. I was someone
who had loved three persons who had been told by a stranger that they were all mad."

Ludwig's study was received with predictable outrage
by the Freudians. He was however, a legitimate
*Menschenkenner,* a writer of best selling biographies and
an honored member of the same cognoscenti the Freudians
hailed for their insights. Through his insight, Ludwig had
perceived the same shallowness that other acute observers
had detected when Freud's magnetism failed to work.

Another disillusioned visitor was the late Professor
Gordon W. Allport.[3] On the street car taking him toward
Bergasse 19, a little boy had behaved in an obsessive
manner and made quite a scene about possible infection
from germs on the dirty seats. Allport described the boy's
behavior to Freud, as one psychologist would to another,
to initiate discussion.

"And was that little boy you?" Freud asked, as he
"fixed his very therapeutic eyes" upon Allport.

The early fifties heralded two remarkable events in
Freudiana: Publication of the long lost Fliess letters which
exposed their sordid history, and the appearance of Ernest
Jones' definitive and official biography. The Fliess affair,
culminating in treachery and bitterness, attended with
the suicide of Weininger and the revelation of Freud's
hatred for Breuer, his greatest benefactor, seriously damaged his reputation, at least in the eyes of the realistic.

But it is the really stupendous work of Ernest Jones
which supplies the vital information needed to appraise
Freud's personality. Only through Jones is it possible to
get the real flavor of the man and to sense the confluences

of his drives. But to really appreciate the work of Jones, a glimpse of this man's amazing personality will also be rewarding.

Jones and Freud were alike in many respects, despite a wide variance in their environments and origins. Jones was also the slender, wiry type, possessed of fantastic sources of energy; a really accomplished and superb writer, fanatic in his beliefs and at times, not too scrupulous. He had excellent organizational ability; was a good hater, very ambitious and also had an excellent medical training. Eventually he ran afoul of the medical establishment, as did Freud.

Jones' parents, however, were both literate and highly intelligent and his circumstances spared him the agonizing poverty that was Freud's unhappy lot. Another important difference was that Jones really loved medicine and had been an excellent physician keenly ambitious to succeed in the profession. The injustices he suffered from the medical hierarchy, due in part to his own lack of tact and conceit as he freely admitted, were really cruel and not the fictions that Freud nourished.

*Free Associations,* the autobiography of Ernest Jones,[4] is frank and very revealing and far more honest than Freud's autobiographical attempts. Jones, unlike Freud, was a man of the world sexually. For years he lived with a woman who was not entirely healthy and took excellent care of her until he decided she needed psychoanalysis. He then brought her to Freud, a fatal step, for the Great One advised severing their relationship. In such cases, his own jealousy must be considered, for Jones was obviously a valuable recruit and the woman was a rival influence.

Throughout his life, Jones relates, he never was free of neural pain. This must be considered in connection with his bursts of temper, and his somewhat irascible and contentious personality. He was also a master of invective and attacked, as did Freud, without identifying the person he attacked.

Freud and Jones were brothers under the skin, both

prone toward inordinate snooping and prying. Bernays[5] had had occasion to resent Jones for such tactics. His role in fomenting Freud's animus toward Jung has already been recounted. The tragedy of Jones' life, as also with Freud, was their rejection by the medical profession. Both worked themselves up into implacable hatreds and animosities that endured all their lives.

In the case of Jones, his career as a physician was doomed from the start because of his various scrapes with the medical authorities. In one case he was accused of sexual advances toward an emotionally disturbed, adolescent girl patient and was jailed overnight but acquitted at his trial. This case had all the earmarks of a plot against him and despite his acquittal, he came to despair of attaining any respectable status as a physician.

It can be imagined then how he was stirred when he learned of psychoanalysis, whose autonomy freed him from the bonds of the medical hierarchy and opened up a glamorous career permitting free indulgence to his Bohemian, anti-social propensities.

Jones was the ideal recruit for Freud, for he became bound to him by desperation, knowing that psychoanalysis was his last chance for fame and success. In his worship of Freud, Jones blinded himself to the humiliations, indignities and contempt Freud characteristically displayed toward anyone in his power. Still, Jones could not blind himself completely and his monumental biography is replete with details of Freud's malice and lack of principle.

In his introduction to Freud's case history (biography) Jones reveals the mental gyrations that permitted his ambivalent worshipful-realism. His "hero worshipping propensities," Jones claimed, had been "worked through" before he had met Freud. Besides, he rationalized, Freud's extraordinary personal integrity would not permit presenting "an idealized portrait of someone remote from humanity." Then Jones reached the depths of insipidity with this whopper:

"His claim to greatness, indeed, lies largely in the honesty and courage with which he struggled and overcame his own inner difficulties and emotional conflicts by means which have been of inestimable value to others."

Under the spell of this delusion of his recovery, Jones presents the evidence of Freud's disturbed thinking. This is typical:

"When . . . Freud found in himself previously unknown attitudes towards his parents, he felt immediately that they were not peculiar to himself and that he had discovered something about human nature in general; Oedipus, Hamlet and the rest soon flashed across his mind."

Actually this proves that Freud was only intent on spreading his own madness, (mother-incest, parricidal hate) to make the world share his guilt. His life work consequently was to degrade human motivation. To achieve that, he also had to denigrate science, professional ethics, logic and just about every system of thought in order to promote his delusions. The basis for his presentation of Oedipal motivations as a common human characteristic was merely his feeling that "previously unknown attitudes toward his parents . . . were not peculiar to himself," and with characteristic ingenuity and gall, this was advanced as a great discovery for which the world should reward him with fame and glory.

This Oedipal discovery occurred to Freud during the period of his greatest travail, the period, Jones wrote, roughly comprising the nineties in which he suffered from a "considerable psycho-neurosis." Though he continued working with "little sign of neurotic manifestations to his surroundings . . . his sufferings were at times very intense and for those ten years there could have been only occasional intervals when life seemed worth living. He paid heavily for the gifts he bestowed upon the world, and the world was not very generous in its rewards." (The martyr myth).

By representing Freud as relieved of his psychoneurosis, despite the considerable evidences he presented himself that it persisted throughout his life, Jones displayed a sad deterioration in his diagnostic ability.

Such blindness to Freud's chronic emotional instability
is common among the mine run of Freudians, especially
if they lacked medical training. But Ernest Jones had
proven himself a competent physician and had been
privileged to work with some of the best physicians in
England. His hypnotic subjugation by Freud probably
accounts for his blindness, as this worshipful passage illus-
trates:

"He was the soul of honor and never deviated
from the highest standards of ethical behavior or
from those of professional probity . . . He was one
of those rare spirits that transcend the smallness
of life and thus show us the picture of real greatness."

Five pages further on:

"On the other hand , oddly enough, Freud was
not a man who found it easy to keep someone else's
secrets. He had indeed the reputation of being distinctly indiscreet."

Whereupon, Jones let many cats out of the bag, reminding first that his feud with Fliess started with such an
indiscretion; that Freud displayed this "unexpected trait"
by blabbing away the confessions of colleagues, "which
he should not have." Jones professed excusing his Master
on the grounds that carrying around these secret confessions imposed a painful burden and he relieved himself
by confiding in one "whose discretion he could trust." The
tension incurred in preserving secrets, Jones alibied, was
relieved through betraying these secrets.

A typical such indiscretion involved James Strachey,
of whom Jones had written a not very complimentary
letter to Freud. Soon after Strachey was on his couch,
Freud dug up the letter and read it aloud to him. On
another occasion, Jones confided to Freud that a patient
he had sent to him was addicted to morphium. Freud
promised to keep Jones' confidence from the patient, but
it was "not long" Jones revealed, "before I received a furious letter from the patient complaining of my action."

This dangerous inability to preserve a confidence, typical of gossipy, overtalkative individuals, would be indica-

tive of a serious derangement in a professional man whose
work in probing into the innermost secrets of humanity
demanded respecting confidences. That Freud was
deranged, Jones could not charge, yet he presents many
proofs of his disorientation, consequent from his intimacy
with the mentally disturbed and endless preoccupation
with mental aberrations.

In connection with a patient Jones knew intimately
whom Freud was treating "before the war," Jones stated
he would come across instance after instance where he
(Freud) was believing statements "which I knew to be
certainly untrue and also, incidentally, refusing to believe
things that were as certainly true."

Unfortunately Jones does not supply details concerning
the untruths Freud believed or the truths he denied, except
for a case related to him (Jones) by Joan Riviere while
she was in analysis with Freud. One morning he fumed
to her that an English patient he had seen that morning
bitterly complained over ill-treatment by an Ipswich analyst. Riviere told him there was no analyst by that name
in Ipswich or elsewhere, but Freud refused to believe and
continued his tirade.

Shortly afterwards Freud received a letter from one
of his disciples that he was sending him a patient with
paranoid indications who was fond of inventing wild tales
of persecution by her doctors. Freud's willingness to
believe her was but another indication of his genius, Jones
fatuously contended, for a will to believe in the improbable
and unexpected was the only way, as Heraclitus advised,
to discover new truths. Though his judgment was seriously
affected, Jones went on, and even ridiculous at times,
"it also enabled him dauntlessly to face the unknown and
thus to open up new fields of knowledge that had remained
closed to more judicial but pedestrian judgments."

Despite these evidences of faulty professional judgment, Jones discloses that Freud was quite shrewd in
money matters. On one occasion his nephew cabled him
a guarantee of $10,000 for six months work here. Freud
refused and made a detailed and masterly business calcu-

lation to prove he would lose money on the deal. He was also quite shrewd about foreign exchange and deposited his moneys in a Dutch bank account as did many Austrians.

Freud was a driver; a hard task master as relentless upon others as he was upon himself. Rank was his work horse, burdened with many menial tasks and so overworked in the early twenties when the tempo of the movement became furious, Jones acknowledges it must have been a factor in his subsequent "mental breakdown."

Jones takes credit for the formation of the "Committee" which Hanns Sachs attributed to Freud. Sachs left little doubt that the Committee was formed for purposes of security and surveillance. Jones attributed a more lofty aim to it, as a form of mental hygiene or preventive psychotherapy to assure that analysts retained their "insight into the workings of the unconscious (which) presupposes a high degree of mental stability. It turned out, alas, that only four of us were."

The four mentally stable were, Eitington, Sachs Jones and Abraham with Freud as the master stabilizer. Of these four, Sachs and Eitington could be classified as the most docile of stooges. To attribute great mental stability to them is farcical for at no time did they display anything but a complete and abject subservience to the Great One.

The two independents, Rank and Ferenczi, Jones charged "developed psychotic manifestations that revealed themselves in, among other ways, a turning away from Freud and his doctrines. The seeds of a destructive psychosis, invisible for so long, at last germinated."

Ferenczi's "destructive psychosis," eventually expressed itself in the observation that Freud had "no more insight than a small boy." According to Jones, "Rank once jokingly remarked that Freud distributed references to other analysts' writings on the same principle the Emperor distributed decorations, on the mood and fancy of the moment."

Jones himself was often the target of his idol's animadversions. Freud nagged him about neglecting his correspondence after receiving complaints from some Viennese analysts. When Jones protested that he was very prompt and explained his system of dating and numbering every paragraph in a letter to induce the complainants to reply promptly, it was but in vain. Freud continued to harp about it and expressed a hope he would improve.

Freud once accused Jones in a letter of having sexual relations with a patient. This was a distortion as the patient had really professed a love for Jones. On another occasion, Freud accused Jones of malice toward his daughter Anna and requested that he stop his "campaign" against her. In another instance when the dispute over lay analysis was raging, Jones contended he advised omitting three strong sentences by Eitington in a booklet on lay analysis, to avoid antagonizing their American cohorts.

Freud then accused Jones of fostering rancor and dispute. "Such a complete travesty of my reconciling aims was evidence of Freud's suspicion that I was opposed to lay analysis," Jones wrote, "he could never understand midway positions such as mine was and still is."

Jones has included so much evidence of Freud's malice as to justify a suspicion that his biography was a means of venting his own grievances against him. Despite his many rhapsodies about Freud's nobility of character, the simultaneous inclusion of so much damaging information is significant. If Freud had one salient fault, it was a complete lack of loyalty or respect for others. He had evinced this over and over again, toward his parents, toward his siblings, toward Breuer and toward his disciples. He was singularly lacking in feeling toward others as Jones so often proved. The following example justifies a suspicion Jones would overlook nothing discreditable to Freud, no matter how trivial:

In 1928, the American psychoanalysts were furious about a charlatan who advertised himself as a qualified colleague because he had studied with Freud, Jung and Adler. He had indeed been referred by Freud to the Vienna Psychoanalytic Institute and received some training there. The New York branch was incensed because the charlatan had capitalized upon this association. They were in "bad enough odor" themselves at the time, despite their medical qualifications so that the intruder was particularly obnoxious, they complained.

Freud "merely shrugged his shoulders," over their complaints, which he thought trivial at most. " 'Anyhow,' " Jones quoted him, " 'the man knows more about psychoanalysis than before he came to Vienna.' "

The most appalling evidence of Freud's malice is the publication of *Moses and Monotheism* in 1939 when the Nazi persecution of Jews was at its height. A more inopportune time for issuing so superfluous and unnecessary a study could hardly be imagined, and again indicates his pathological fund of hatred for Freud was capable of nursing a grudge for years.

The impulse for revenge against his own people, may have originated in 1933 when Eitington had emigrated to Jerusalem and attempted to induce the Hebrew University to establish a chair on psychoanalysis. J. L. Magnes,[6] director of the University, then wrote to Freud quite courteously that "it would be premature to introduce psychoanalysis before a chair of psychology has been established." He added that the university was searching for suitable candidates and had Kurt Lewin in mind, and deferred to Freud by asking for his recommendations. Freud replied with a typical display of insolence and egomania:

"There is no need to begin the teaching of psychology with traditional academic psychology. On the contrary all applications of psychology to medicine and to the humanities originate from the profound depths of psychoanalysis, while academic psychology has been proven too sterile.

"I see no reason to assume that Professor Kurt Lewin will be the man to carry out the synthesis of psychoanalysis and psychology. Under these circumstances the plan to establish a chair for psychology indicates a barely disguised rejection of psychoanalysis and the University of Jerusalem would thus have followed the example of other

official teaching institutions. It is then comforting to bear
in mind that Dr. Eitington is determined to pursue the
practice of psychoanalysis in Palestine also independent of
the University."

In his ghastly Moses book whose purpose baffled so
many of his followers, Freud inadvertently revealed the
secret of his persuasive technique — arguing by the undis-
provable. His contention that Moses was not a Jew but an
Egyptian, cannot of course be disproved; it is a possibility,
but no more. Hitler was not a German nor was Napoleon a
Frenchman. Therefore Moses may have been other than a
Jew, but after 5,000 years, is it important? However,
Moses was a figure of great spiritual significance to the
Jews and Freud's denigration was typical of his lack of
respect for anything save his own interests.

Jones dwelt on the animosity and animadversion
Freud aroused because of his views on Moses. Professor
Yahuda, a learned Jewish historian, begged Freud not to
publish the book. In November of 1938, a representative of
the Yiddish Scientific Society interviewed Freud who discoursed at length on Moses and acknowledged he had been
warned by Jews not to publish. "But to him the truth was
sacred," Jones throbbed, "and he could not renounce his
rights as a scientist not to voice it."

After publication, Freud was dosed with his own
medicine. A leading Jewish biblical scholar, T.W. Rosmarin, asserted that no one has a right to opinion on Biblical
topics until first acquiring some knowledge of Hebrew,
Egyptian and related languages. Jones was inclined to
admit Freud's guilt in this respect, oblivious to the fact
that he denied the right of anyone to criticize psychoanalysis on similar grounds.

Rosmarin accused Freud of a bitter hatred toward Jews
which fomented his attack upon Moses to deprive them of a
leader. "How remote this malevolent charge is from the
truth there is no need for me to stress," Jones loftily asserted. Nevertheless, he included further adverse and bitter comments from a review of the book by Professor Abraham Yahuda, the man who had vainly implored him not

to publish, whose review ended:

"It seems to me that in these words we hear the voice of one of the most fanatical Christians in his hatred of Israel and not the voice of a Freud who hated and despised such fanatacism with all his heart and strength."

Freud's undeserved reputation as a martyr to the truth screened his innate perfidy, as this ludicrous statement by the learned professor signifies. Despite Freud's publication of a venomous, uncalled for diatribe which his learned critic deplored, he was spared the accusation of congenital misanthropy. The inadequacy of intellectuals for realistic judgment is exemplified by Yahuda's puerile conclusion. Again and again other intellectuals, including Eric Fromm, have been baffled by Freud's Moses study without being able to perceive it as merely a manifestation of his pathological hatred and nothing else.

A glaring example of Freud's duplicity about anti-Semitism is this reference to Jung in his history of his movement:

"He seemed prepared to enter into friendly relations with me and to give up for my sake certain race prejudices which he had so far permitted himself to entertain."

According to an investigator of this invidious statement[7] "No evidence in support of this statement exists in Jung's writings."

It is, however, mystifying why Jung never took the time to deny this insinuation, for he was quite sympathetic to Jews as his very loyal support of Freud testifies. Moreover his biographer Bennett, writes that "Jung was surprised and shocked at Freud's distaste for Jewish analysts — his epithet for them was *Judenbengels* . . . Freud's animosity was perhaps intensified because he wanted a wider basis for the new teaching."

Despite its generally eulogistic tone, the monumental work by Jones produced by so much industry, fluency and devotion deserved a far worthier subject. So much detailed attention to so shallow a personality, repelled many realistic readers. A close-up of Freud was disillusioning; the more he was eulogized, the sorrier he became.

In 1956, Professor Percival Bailey of the University of Illinois, delivered the opening address at the American Psychiatric Convention. His subject was psychoanalysis which he proclaimed was the "greatest hoax of the Twentieth Century," created by Sigmund Freud as occupational therapy for himself. Bailey later incorporated his views in a critical biography with the lacklustre title, *Sigmund the Unserene*[7] to discourage students of psychiatry from embracing psychoanalysis as a profession. His discouraging view of Freud and his system may have contributed to the significant decline in applicants in recent years.

"More than a religion," Professor Bailey states, "the psychoanalytic movement has become political. Its adepts have become a political guild which aspires to dominate psychiatric education in this country. In two recent instances, they threatened to resign in mass from a department of psychiatry if a man who was biologically oriented was put at the head of it. In one case, they succeeded in blocking an appointment. The psychoanalysts aim still higher. Ernest Jones wrote that he hoped to live to see the day when any candidate to a position in the foreign service would be obliged first, to undergo a personal analysis."*

Late in the fifties, I edited and published the late Coyne H. Campbell's *Induced Delusions*. As a dissident Doctor Campbell was unique; he did not embrace another branch of Freudism but devoted himself to psychiatry based on biological principles. He also became certified as an internist so that his divorce from the Freudian ideology was final and complete.

We had many conversations in which his anger and deep disgust for the movement rose to the surface. It became my impression that he was highly suggestible and his induction into the movement was against his will, maneuvered after constant nagging, high pressure salesmanship and warnings he would go nowhere in the profession unless he took up psychoanalysis. He was a highly desirable candidate to the Freudians because of his brilliant scholarship and they could not rest until he was

*The effects of a personal analysis upon a diplomat can be apprised from the William C. Bullitt collaboration with Freud in their biographical denigration of President Woodrow Wilson, (Houghton, Mifflin, 1966).*

snared.

His renunciation of psychoanalysis was very traumatic and also exposed him to the hatred and virulence of his former Freudian brethren. Despite this, he became head of the department of psychiatry at the University of Oklahoma and very successful in practice. Reviving his trauma in publishing his book, may have brought about a severe depression in which he took his own life.

In the sixties, Freudian prestige became increasingly threatened with the advances in the biochemical approaches that Doctor Sargant attested were successful in Europe. At a seminar to celebrate Franz Alexander's seventieth birthday in 1961, "the father of American psychoanalysis," as he was characterized in the *Los Angeles Times,* warned that while the physiology of the brain was of "the greatest theoretical significance, neurophysiology will never bury psychology, it will only complement it . . . the expectations to reduce the universe relentlessly to the laws of physics and chemistry are as hopeless as they are senseless."

Conceding that some pharmaceuticals could render patients more approachable, he contended that rarely would they cure. His deep antagonism to biochemical approaches was apparent despite the double talk, and was espoused under the guise of freedom of will. Alexander deplored biochemical approaches as a departure "from the spirit of the renaissance — individual freedom — toward central planning."

This pronunciamento had issued from the protegee of the greatest of all central planners; a man who would reduce all human motivations to mother incest and parricide and devoted his considerable energies to overcoming all resistance to this obsession.

Fortunately the "spirit of the renaissance" burst forth dramatically from a most unusual source, a genuine Freudian psychoanalyst, retiring as president of the American Psychoanalytical Association, namely Judd Marmor. In his farewell address of 1966, Doctor Marmor announced he was abandoning his analytic practice of over twenty years to direct a psychiatric clinic. He published his reasons for this in "Psychoanalysis at the Crossroad,"[9] written with an unfreudian frankness and directness, reminiscent of Freud's remarkable letter of 1897 relinquishing belief in his "neurotica."

Doctor Marmor confessed almost complete disillusionment and questioned the most hoary tenets of the faith. Of the combination of research and therapy, he stated:

"There is no good reason *apriori* why a technique of investigation should be a good method of therapy. I suspect that it was largely the historical accident that Freud was attempting to earn a living as a psychiatric practitioner that drove him to utilize his investigative tool as a therapeutic instrument. Little wonder that Freud said in later years that although his initial problem was getting patients his eventual difficulty was in getting them to leave him."

(Compare his directives, advising that a patient attempting to break off treatment should be warned that an uncompleted analysis was like an unfinished surgical operation.)

On Freud: Hostility to his views forced Freud into "dedicated militancy," and he equated theoretical disagreement with personal hostility or disloyalty.

On training analyses: A rigid hierarchy of training institutes existed; candidates were dropped when doubts arose because these doubts were regarded as "resistance." The institutes taught Freud as "talmudic history", rather than living, changing concepts. Institutes taught ego theory and libidinal concepts with a "degree of emotional fervor that belongs within the confines of a religious organization rather than in the halls of science."

It is repetitive to continue citing Doctor Marmor as much that he said has already been set down here. He warned his colleagues ominously that they must either strive "to exert a paramount influence on modern psychiatric thought or they will gradually recede into an unimportant sidestream by virtue of failure to keep abreast of modern developments in the behavioral sciences."

As for new candidates, he deplored that many of "the brightest young minds in psychiatry who for the past twenty years flocked to psychoanalytic institutes for training are turning their eyes in other directions."

One reason for this disaffection which Marmor did not bring out, was the ever increasing length of training analyses. The day an applicant can enter practice and recoup his investment in a training analysis recedes further and further, just as an analysis can continue stretching out interminably.

In this respect, K.A. Fisher, writing in a 1967 issue of the *Psychoanalytic Review* observed:

"In the decades since Freud the acceptable duration of analysis has become longer and longer. Ten, twelve and even fifteen years of treatment have been reported. In the twenties, a didactive analysis was 100 hours. By the sixties, especially in orthodox analytic institutes, 700 to 800 hours appear to be standard. From cursory inspection one suspects that from 1500 to 2000 hours are not unknown."

In 1967, from his grave Freud himself contributed to the accelerating decline of his dogma. His posthumous collaboration with a former patient and U.S. Ambassador, William C. Bullitt, in a psychological study of President Woodrow Wilson was very poorly received and reveals the unfortunate consequences of statesmen undergoing analysis, as Ernest Jones so grandiloquently predicted might become obligatory.

The book seemed poisoned with the same hate which evoked *Moses and Monotheism*. Years before in an interview with Max Eastman, Freud had denigrated Wilson as a "fool, perhaps the silliest fool of the century." He was not immune from the same blind prejudices of his rioting fellow Viennese in 1921 who blamed Wilson and the United States for all their troubles as Oberndorf had reported to him.

Like a bomb set to explode when the time was ripe, the Wilson study appeared in 1966.[10] It could not have been detonated sooner because Freud's escape from the Nazi's was engineered with the American help of Bullitt, FDR and considerable cash, so that there was a risk of offending American sensibilities by attacking an American president.

Nevertheless the study was so offensive it even antagonized genuine, card carrying Freudians. One analyst, unnamed, ridiculed it as "gibberish" in *Science News,* of January 28, 1967. Another, also anonymous, thought Freud could have been more "sophisticated" for his naivete was "unbelievable and the book poorly written."

Freud's superlative readability was lacking. Bullitt alone may have written it and then submitted it to Freud for a polishing he never rendered. Years later his heirs, ever avid for something to publish to perpetuate his fame, seized upon it as saleable.

Psychoanalyzing a man he had never met, from relying upon the biased viewpoint of a former associate, and applying two concepts being questioned by skeptical Freudians, the libido theory and Oedipal motivations, backfired badly. These concepts had won acceptance by endless repetition but eventually even automatic repetition fails to work. Eventually an image also must fade, no matter how carefully it is polished.

Leon Salzman, a prominent analyst now advocating defreudianization, proclaims that a new image of the psychoanalyst is being formed as a result of "serious scientific efforts to frame psychodynamic concepts out of research, experience and observation, not conjecture and flights of poetic fancy."[11] This is typical Freudianese, however, couched as usual in vague generalitites. The necessity to frame concepts out of "research, experience and observations" instead of flights of fancy, implies that Freud did not base his conjectures on sound scientific work, just as his enemies always contended.

In these days of Madison Avenue technology, the image is everything; charisma is payola. Freud's image lost glamour through over-exposure. The Fliess letters, the over-intimacy of Jones in his ambivalent biography and finally the Wilson fiasco, was highly damaging. Salzman advocated a change of image because it is presently "in bad shape and somewhat grotesque." Psyching Salzman's remarks, his underlying message would seem to be:

"We can't be stuck with Freud's tarnished and faded image. To psychoanalyze a man without putting him on the couch is bad business. If it can be done that way, who needs us?"

The reform is well underway. According to Leon Saul, high in the Freudian hierarchy, analytic sessions are supplemented by "direct physiological measurements . . . and include records of respiration, pulse, blood pressure and psychogalvanic reflexes, temperature changes and electroencephalograms." However, let us not get too enthusiastic about these remarkable advances which now bring psychoanalysts up to circa 1900, for Leon Saul adds:

"Most of these studies are only now in progress and important results have not yet been reported. Their value will depend upon the ability to describe the mental states with an exactness comparable to that of the physiological measurements."

Reading between the lines, it would seem that the analysts still follow Freud in conducting research and therapy simultaneously, but having found dreams worthless in diagnosis, they are taking to laboratory instruments whose recordings can be just as whimsically interpreted as dreams. Medical diagnosticians have a gobbledegook all their own to interpret electroencephalograms and cardiograms. Cases are well known of patients whose cardiograms indicated no disorder, who dropped dead of heart failure only hours after leaving the physician's office.

Approaching the seventies, the Freudian movement went Hollywood. "Freud" directed by Walter Huston reached film but flopped at the box office. Nor did changing the title to "Her Secret Passion," improve the take. Freud was played by one of Hollywood's least animated actors, returning to the screen after suffering a serious accident from which he had evidently not recovered for he died soon after.

Playing Freud in the Breuer period depicted would have demanded wide gyrations of emotion this actor could not attain, hence Freud did not come off very well. He was portrayed as an idealistic searcher, perplexed by the problems his patients presented and anxiously discussing them with his wife. Since there is little indication she ever understood a word he said, this gave matters a comical twist.

The consultant for the film was an English Freudian, David Stafford-Clark. The material was quite authentic and included a scene in which Freud, at age three or four, saw his mother nude, which he later confessed "stimulated" his libido. In lay terms, it means he experienced an erection.

Breuer was very well played in the film. In one scene, he is depicted as declining Freud's request to treat his neurosis. This seems hardly likely as Breuer was a very sympathetic person and thought very highly of Freud at that time. Still, it may have been true and Breuer's refusal may have been due to his repugnance for the intense intimacies of psychological treatment. The patient whose "secret passion" inspired the title for the film, had once been Breuer's and it was he who had been her secret love.

When his wife became jealous, Breuer referred the girl to Freud. She also had a secret yen to become a courtesan and the highlight of the film is Freud rescuing her from a brothel in the nick of time, a lá Hollywood. During their walk back to her home, she invited him to become her first professional client, for free, just for the practice. On the late, late show, this scene, alas, has been deleted.

*Finis* is reached very dramatically when Freud expounds his infantile sexuality theory before the Vienna Medical Society. As he spoke, a rising crescendo of angry shouts assails him. A doctor who was the spitting image of Karl Marx, actually spits in front of Freud when his discourse closed. A number of physicians then rise to express their loathing. One asks Breuer directly if he believes Freud's theories.

Breuer rises to express his faith in Freud's integrity but when he is pressed to answer the question, he admits that he does not believe in his sexual dogma. This was, of course true, though Breuer's disavowal may not have been brought out so dramatically, but it could account for Freud's hatred, instantaneous when his sexuality was rejected. On the surface, he remained polite; Breuer continued to refer patients to him and he continued to remain in debt to him financially for another ten years.

In his corrsepondence with Fliess, Freud revealed his bitter animosity to Breuer, his greatest benefactor, while expressing only praise and gratitude in his published writings. Despite his idolatry, Jones was compelled to call attention to Freud's duplicity in the official biography.

## CHAPTER 9

# The Passionate Mind

*"Imaginative writers are valuable colleagues and their testimony is to be rated very highly, because they have a way of knowing many of the things between heaven and earth which are not dreamed of in our philosophy."*

Early in 1971 the radio blared that Irving Stone's biographical novel of Sigmund Freud would soon appear. This was astounding; one would think that Ernest Jones' monumental three volumes had exhausted the subject. Moreover, why Irving Stone of the saccharine Madison Avenue style, so incongruous considering Freud's sour personality and morbid predilections? Was he another analysand recouping the staggering costs of his encouchment with a paean to the Pied Piper of Vienna?

Irving Stone then could be another Lucy Freeman, tediously espousing the Freudian enlightenment. Lucy may hold the world's record for interminable analyses with more than twenty years logged on various couches. Her *Fight Against Fears,* published in the early fifties, invited the world to share the glorious victory she had won in her stirring psychic battles. Over two decades later, the fight still rages, but it is certain none of her various analysts have suffered a scratch in the fray.

Irving Stone's books have sold in the millions; he outranks Lucy Freeman as a best seller, though not in Dun

& Bradstreet's for the lady has inherited her attorney father's millions, some of it garnered from Mafia clients. The day's news (Feb. 19, 1973) carries the obituary of Frank Costello, well known power in the underworld, who was a client of Lucy Freeman' father. Stone is also well heeled and reputed as having a million in accrued royalties with his publishers, which is being spread over the years to save taxes.

Stone's entry into the lists of Freud's biographers hints the plight of psychoanalysis is desperate. The Wilson fiasco badly damaged Freud's prestige; something was needed to refurbish his image. *The Passions of the Mind* was possibly another promotional gimmick, another appeal to the popular imagination which had won fame and fortune for Freud.

The overexposure, the many sickening details of his personality which Jones had released, needed glossing over. What could be more helpful than Irving Stone's soothing style which had attracted millions of readers? Through him, an entirely new audience would be reached, a new generation who would accept Freud as a hero. Stone's journalistic style was highly successful, and though not distinguished as literature, his authorship guaranteed wide circulation.

But you cannot please everyone. The reviewer of *The Passions of the Mind* for the *Atlantic Monthly,* quailed at Stone's one-sided presentation which had excised all of Freud's "warts" in portraying him as a Frank Merriwell of the psyche. He quoted several mawkish passages to illustrate his point.

It was not so with the *Los Angeles Times.* Their reviewer went into ecstasies over Stone's meticulous research which synthesized "in lucid language, the complex tangle of science, art, personality implicit in the story of Freud (and ) something more. It renders the source and meld of experience, growth and perceptions, which go into creativity. It is not only biography but an adventure of the intellect and imagination."

Whew!

*Time,* however, was rather blasè about Stone's opus. Its reviewer snidely accused Freud of carrying on with Tante Minna. (She was his wife's old maid sister who lived in his household for many years and occasionally accompanied Freud unchaperoned on vacation jaunts while Mrs. Freud stayed home with the siblings.)

After reading these reviews, Stone did not seem a likely source of new clues to Freud's inexpressible, terrifying *numinosum.* Still, as a layman who had never before published anything of a psychological nature, he did promise a new and curious slant. So I bought and started to read his gushing, which included many homey touches on Viennese life and recipes. Not only did Stone write a biography, but a travelogue and cookbook as well, the latter probably the work of Mrs. Stone, to insure everyone getting their money's worth. Readers probably wrote Mrs. Stone for such recipes as:

Kraut mit Rahm. A finely shredded cabbage, cooked with sour cream and sprinkled with caraway seed.

Gugelhupf. A yeast cake in the form of a cone, about ten inches high, made with raisins, almonds and lots of custard.

As I read the book upon which Stone either decided or was induced to "lavish his talents as a biographical novelist and five years of tireless research and writing," (to quote the jacket blurb) it was often hard to believe that Sigmund Freud was the subject. There is a shallowness, a superficiality and a peculiar detachment which prevent any intimation the author was glorifying a monster. The relationship with Fliess, for example, is mentioned so casually as to be impossible to suspect its tragic implications. Fliess is denigrated professionally and lampooned as pompous, conceited and dangerously careless. Stone relates that a patient referred by Freud upon whom he operated almost died of an infection because a surgical sponge was left in the incision.

On the credit side, is the evidence of Stone's indefatigable research, the amassing of so much that is new and revealing. Despite his gushing, he is not only readable, but in comparison with the gobbledegook that passes for professional contributions, he is interesting and entertaining. He is an excellent journalist and if one disregards how he says it, but concentrates upon what he says, the book is a mine of valuable details. Stone also corroborates Krafft-Ebing's observation that the psychiatrist's outlook is determined by his subjective conditioning. In psyching Freud and selecting for elaboration that what he thought was significant, Stone unwittingly also wrote his own autobiography.

In this age of miraculous communication, when *The Passions of the Mind* appeared, it was possible not only to read it, but also to see the author. In the promotion of his book, Stone appeared on the Virginia Graham TV show in Hollywood. Modest and commonplace in appearance, he spoke in a subdued and undistinguished tone. Gushy Miss Graham's first question, based on the assumption he had been or still was in analysis, brought a surprising denial, on the grounds that he had never felt "the need for it," married as he still was both to the same editor-wife and the same publisher for almost forty years. This implied that long, compatible relationships precluded the existence of neuroses. Stone also volunteered the autobiographical tidbit that their marriage dowry was a $250.00 advance on his first accepted manuscript which had united him both with his wife-editor and his publisher in a serene association eventually leading to riches and glory.

Stone was undoubtedly right in believing a steady, practical man does not need analysis. In fact, a practical man is unsuitable for he could certainly manifest great resistance over today's fees. Freud would probably never have reserved any couch time for unneurotic Stone, cordial though his heirs have been in giving him free access to his archives.

The next question oozed from the libido of a glamorous and much married singer who had preceded Stone on the program and stayed for the interview. Her question betrayed her psyche worked something like this:

"Married to the same woman for thirty-seven years, what a square! I wonder if the guy ever played around? But I can't ask him that, not on TV." Instead, she asked: "How about Freud's affair with Tante Minna?"

Who could blame her for thinking along the same lines as the reviewer for *Time?* What could be more natural than assuming that a man who continually advocated complete freedom of the libido would have wanted to enjoy his sister-in-law's company to the fullest during their jaunts?

Stone quickly rectified this erroneous assumption, by affirming that Freud's sex life had always been pure. He had been a virgin at marriage (age thirty) and in his entire life had carnally known only one woman, his wife. Stone went further to attest that Freud even had a puritanical streak and related that when he was a student in Paris (about 1885) he was shocked when he saw ladies in the Louvre staring unabashedly at the male genitalia on sculptures.

"Have these people no shame?" Freud wrote home.

Suddenly the conversation lulled. It would have been a good spot for a commercial. Freud's image as a daring sexologist, baseing his findings upon his own libidinal exploits with Tante Minna was badly smudged. How had a bashful, prudish, one-woman man become a world authority on sex? And, come to think of it, was it not possible that Tante Minna's libido was in spinsterish cold storage and she too was immune from carnal lusts?

The gorgeous singer then trilled an ominous note: Women's Lib opposed Freud's theory of penis envy. Stone acknowledged this opposition, but contended penis envy was a bi-sexual phenomenon. We are not all 100 percent male or female, he pontificated, but a mixture of both sexes. A seventy-thirty mix can be normal; the danger point is fifty-fifty. This clearly infers that only some women, those with high masculine components, are penis envious. However, that was not Freud, for he contended that penis envy is universal in all women.

Stone neglected to mention or may not have been aware

that Freud himself had quite a feminine bearing, indicating dangerous reading on the bisexual meter. The bisexual theory originated with Fliess, but Stone sounded as if it were Freud's idea. This is understandable, for once Freud incorporated an idea into his system it became his original discovery, which no one before ever had the genius to discern. J.F. Herbart, an Austrian (1776-1841), had written extensively on the unconscious mind and advanced theories quite similar to Freud's, but had never found wide acceptance. It was Freud's achievement to gain credibility for Herbart's ideas in giving them a twist all his own by incorporating his sexology.

When the TV interview turned to Freud's strenuous fight for recognition, Stone blamed the Church for its opposition and for instigating Jung's alienation. This was indeed a blooper, contradicting Stone's own text, for Jung was a born heretic, the last man to be intimidated by Church authority. He had left Freud when he heard the same authoritarian tone commanding him to believe in the sanctity of the Oedipus complex.

In closing Stone's appearance, Virginia Graham put in a friendly plug for *The Passions of the Mind* as a great book to learn about dreams, thus heralding a bizarre development. Psychology and other sciences can now be brought down to the grass roots level, to be discussed through media catering to the general public in an atmosphere of ballyhoo, salesmanship, gossip and showmanship. Freudology thereby become subject to the vagaries of public opinion, the mass thinking that Jung termed the "collective unconscious," but also termed more realistically as mob psychology.

This attempt to popularize Freud through Irving Stone is one of the most grotesque in the frenetic history of psychoanalysis. It connotes a severe loss of professional respect by resorting to addressing the general public. It also exposes the hollowness of Freud's contention that only the analyzed are in a position to judge, for Stone never was in analysis, yet he received the wholehearted cooperation of Ernest Freud, keeper of the holy archives,

Sigmund's "son"* Anna and in all probability, nephew Edward L. Bernays, who to this day endows studies and researches conducted by Freudians.

The Freud interests, including the family and the professional organizations are certainly keenly aware of the value of publicity and the need to keep Freud's image brightly polished. The status of psychoanalysis is grounded on Freud's fame; his disciples have little to advertise of their own progress. Analyses are still interminable affairs, dragging on and on as long as payments continue. The reputation of analysts for avarice, indolence, and failing even to listen, has deteriorated even further in recent years. Reports now current of sexual intercourse with patients charged on the bill as treatments, keep mounting. Favorable publicity is needed to counteract these gruesome developments, hence Irving Stone.

Reading Stone's contribution dissipates many myths about Freud, despite his panegyrical, eulogistic style. It has all the emotional fervor of advertising copy, but enjoys an unusual distinction because Stone was never emotionally involved with psychoanalysis. Like most of his biographical novels, *The Passions of the Mind* was compiled through research, without personal contact with his subject. Though his goal was popularity and best sellerdom, he does not distort facts, nor did he suppress them.

Above all, Stone dissipates the myth that Freud bequeathed to the world an abstruse, highly complex science and interpretive technique. In the few years he was occupied with the dogma, Stone appears to have mastered it quite well, without the necessity of prostrating himself upon a couch. His writings compare favorably with professional contributions though it does suffer in comparison with Freud's superb literary craftsmanship, which also benefited from excellent translations. Stone also suffers in comparison with Ernest Jones in literary ability, for he had Freud declaiming to everyone in sight, including his wife and Tante Minna, as if on a podium, in stilted academese. That was not like Freud; he spoke just as

*Freud aroused much amusement by referring to Anna as his "son", for she alone of his children became a psychoanalyst. It is generally suspected that his spinster "son" never could substantiate his libido theory in real life.

he wrote, simply, tersely and with a fine turn for every phrase.

The following excerpt, describing Freud's preparations for a conclave with his admirers (Salzburg, 1908) is a fair example of Stone's style and devotion to minutiae:

"Sigmund rose early the next morning, took breakfast in his room, had the hotel barber cut his dark rich hair and trim the short sideburns, graying chin beard and handsome mustache. He then donned the new gray woven suit he had had made for the occasion and the white linen shirt, the collar coming down to a V with a black bow tie tucked under its wings, and the stiff white cuffs held together by the cuff links Martha (his wife) had given him for his last birthday. He then glanced at himself in the mirror of the wardrobe before he left the room, decided that he did not look old for fifty-two, and that although he sometimes thought of death, and imagined that it had a predetermined pattern, he was in a sense really just beginning life."

Stone does give a hint of a passionate mind, of the cosmos, of death, life, aging, rebirth, together with excessive vanity, foppery, impending triumph arriving quite late, but still welcome at fifty-two. Though the prologue had been ridicule, disappointment, the frustration of vainly anticipating fame in an agony of expectation, *Der Tag* was finally at hand. As Stone could have added, Freud took a last look into the mirror, pleased with his appearance, he made a final brush of his new suit, carefully closed the door and was off to make his entrance before Jung, Brill, Jones and others, the cynosure of their admiring eyes.

In reading Stone, one becomes staggered by the vast amount of material he sifted through, in all probability Freud's voluminous notes, the products of his amazing industry and energy, written every night after long hours of daily consultations. When selecting for publication, Freud omitted or censored much that he wrote in the fever of creation or fighting off drowsiness.

For example, Freud proclaimed that all neurotics suffer from disturbed sexual functioning and freeing the libido, restores mental health and Stone reveals the remarkable case which inspired that opinion. This "most miraculous success" (Freud's own words) was attained before psychoanalysis with a man in his thirties. Believing he could not help the man through office treatment, Freud advised confinement in a sanitarium.

After his first week there, Freud was amazed at his patient's improvement; his facial tics and stuttering were vanishing and he was able to concentrate, an inability which had cost him his job. After three months at the sanitarium with continuing improvement, Freud suggested his patient be discharged. The man became almost violent in refusing to return home. Since the expense was no problem, he was allowed to stay on. Several months later he left for home of his own accord and soon visited Freud in very good health and spirits. Freud asked him how he had effected "such a complete cure." (Note that Freud took no credit for his recovery).

The cure was in the next room, the ex-patient laughingly disclosed. An attractive woman bored with her husband and using the sanitarium to escape, slept with him every night, "the most glorious period of my life," the man exulted. He had come to thank Freud in the belief he had planted the woman next to him for his therapy. Such are the Viennese. Such was also Freud, for he later took credit for the cure, not as a procurer as the man believed, but through suggesting psychoanalysis could effect similar cures.

Another interesting sidelight concerned the celebrated patient with an impotent husband for whom Chrobak, a gynecologist, had prescribed "penis normalis, dosem repetitur." This was another pre-psychoanalytic case Freud wrote about, without disclosing that Chrobak had referred the woman whose condition was considered hopeless, to him. Freud demurred from treating her at first on the ground he could offer nothing but some vaguely cheerful counsel, but did consent to make periodic house calls, which were welcomed and encouraged and scrupulously paid for. After about one hundred visits, Freud terminated his services, unwilling to risk adverse criticism for useless work; so Stone has recorded.

The change in Freud's personality after creating psychoanalysis is clearly startling, for discontinuing seances on the grounds of their futility, became unheard of. In fact, continued seances because their futility insures lasting payment and profit, became routine practice in psychoanalysis.

Stone's biography begins where Freud is betrothed and advised to go into medical practice because his prospects at the University were bleak. Jones pictures Freud as very reluctant to take this step, as he no doubt was, but there is also good reason to believe he got over his dread and eventually even enjoyed his practice. Freud did admit that when he practiced hypnosis he was flattered by being regarded as a "miracle worker."

The Fliess period, also termed the years of "splendid isolation" do not appear as torturing and agonizing as Jones bemoaned under Stone's treatment. True, Freud's practice did fluctuate, but he always managed to earn a living, to take his yearly vacation and sometimes even had more patients than he could handle. According to Stone's findings, he was often referred patients by former teachers and colleagues, thus exploding the myth that they were indifferent to his existence or completely hostile.

Freud's agonized letters to Fliess, bear out his occasional despair and suffering, but his vivid imagination incurs the suspicion he magnified his difficulties. As mentioned, Jung was astounded by the "intensity of his fantasies" of death wishes against him, which made him swoon away. Freud also had a somewhat paranoid attitude about Meynert whom he accused, in his autobiography, of trying to assign some research he suspected was a trap meant to discredit him.

Stone portrays Meynert as a genial, sociable fellow, a little flamboyant but with scarcely any trace of the vindictive. To be sure, when Freud returned from Paris to

declaim so enthusiastically over Charcot's theories,
Meynert ridiculed them. Save for this, Meynert was
friendly, referred patients to him and never refused to
see him. According to Freud, Meynert confessed to him
on his deathbed that he himself was an hysteric and a
drug addict. Without compunction Freud broadcast this
unwitnessed and confidential deathbed confession. In view
of his capacity for intense fantasy, he could very well
have exaggerated or distorted Meynert's last words.

Probably the most glaring case of Freud's lack of high
ethical standards is his bitterness toward Breuer in view
of his many benefactions and his kind treatment, dating
from Freud's student days. He was regarded as one of
the family by the Breuers, almost like a son and visited
the Breuer home on the most intimate terms, to bathe,
change linen and sit at the table. Breuer had also helped
very materially in establishing his practice, collaborated
in *Studies on Hysteria* and his loans commencing with
his student days until he went into practice, eventually
amounted to $2,000, a very considerable sum in those
days.

After Freud went into practice, and offered to start
paying his debt in installments, Breuer generously waved
any payments for the next ten years. In 1898, twelve years
later, Freud offered his first payment of 350 Gulder.
According to Stone, Breuer generously authorized him
to keep that installment as his fee for treating one of
his indigent relatives. Freud kept her under his care for
four years, and then pronounced her relieved of her
neurosis which he claimed had a sexual etiology. He then
sent her to Breuer as a testimonial to his therapeutic
powers. Impressed, Breuer is quoted as saying:

"He may be right after all."

This incident proves that when it served his purposes,
Freud could terminate a case. Treatment extended over
four years however, may have been sufficient to discharge
his debt to Breuer or to reduce it very considerably. That
Freud was capable of such shenanigans, has been born
out. Remember that Adler did not hesitate to call him

a "liar and swindler."

Stone's uniformly panegyrical style can become tedious reading, in view of the fact that his hero's amazing gift of gab concealed the fact he was really a bore, a pesty meddler, egoistic, immune from deep concern for others and saddled with vindictiveness, excessive vanity and bitter jealousies. No matter how thick Stone lays on the treacle, the inevitable truth still emerges: Freud was unethical in his practices. His confession that he had never been a physician "in the proper sense," hints he was aware of his deficiencies.

For example, Freud once treated a sexual pervert who also had a severe phobia about food contamination from the dirty fingers of restaurant employees. The man's perversion was practiced on little girls from families of friends whom he took for overnight stays in country inns.

In one seance, he voiced his disgust about waiters with germ-laden fingers, whereupon Freud blurted:

"Since you have this phobia about germs, aren't you afraid to put your dirty fingers into the vaginas of your little friends?"

The patient sprung from the couch, heatedly denied the perversion that Freud had "guessed" and stormed out, never to return. He also forgot to surrender the carefully washed bills he had prepared for his fees, Stone was careful to mention.

Another violent termination happened with the wife of a very jealous Berlin man. She would come to Vienna for her seances, but one day her husband suddenly appeared at Bergasse 19, broke into Freud's consultation room and forcibly removed his wife from the couch.

These cases illustrate the experiences upon which Freud evolved his technique and directives. The alleged pervert whose aberration Freud had "guessed" had been offended by a blunt interpretation and became a runaway; the type that jeopardized his livelihood. The woman whose husband was jealous he was dependent upon for fees; she also had probably divulged something about Freud's methods to her husband.

In his directives, Freud advised his followers not to render interpretations until the transference was in full bloom. Obviously this would insure ready acceptance of interpretations. Relatives who interfered by demanding results and also balked at the length and expense of treatments were the bane of Freud's existence. He complained bitterly about them in his *General Introduction to Psychoanalysis* and to avoid such interference, he began restricting his practice only to those with independent means. His rule against divulging anything of the analysis to outsiders, and to Freud, anyone was an outsider be it the twin of his patient, meant complete silence. His rule that "telling everything means telling everything" (to me); but to outsiders he decreed telling them nothing means telling them nothing" (about me).

The rule that one's subjectivity determines the selection of material for elaboration is confirmed by Stone's detailed attention to Freud's financial affairs. He accounts for Freud's income, his fees, his debts and expenditures with a bookkeeper's fidelity. Stone majored in economics before taking up writing as a career.

His treatment of Freud's appointment as *professor extraordinarius* aptly displays his subjective bent, for he depicts Freud as a master of self-promotion. In fact, Freud's wily shrewdness for manipulation is dwelt upon with very evident relish and admiration, in far greater detail and probably, with far more accuracy than any other biographer. Ernest Jones suffers badly in comparison to Stone in the matter of his *professor extraordinarius* appointment.

In his anxiety to secure the appointment, comparable to associate professor in the United States and usually a long, complicated business, Freud sought out a socially prominent woman who was under some obligation to him for treating a minor neurologic disorder. The lady had no knowledge of psychoanalysis but her sympathies were deftly played upon and her assistance sought on the strength of Freud's earlier "long years of work in neurology and children's paralyses," after which he mentioned his "newer researches" meaning of course, psychoanalysis.

Despite the lady's earnest efforts, Freud got nowhere until a baroness who had also once been his patient and was very grateful for his cure of her severe headaches, started an enthusiastic campaign in his behalf. She corralled the Minister who passed upon University appointments to plead Freud's case. However, he was equally anxious to secure her assistance to wheedle her aunt into giving a Böcklin to a new art museum which he was in charge of building.

Whereupon the baroness eagerly promised her assistance with the tacit agreement that Freud's appointment would be part of the deal. Though the baroness could not deliver the Böcklin, she kept dangling a painting she owned in front of the Minister. Finally he snatched her bait and agreed to accept it in place of the Böcklin, thus consummating the deal for Freud's appointment. That night Freud wrote one of his last letters to Fliess, sarcastically proclaiming that with the appointment "the role of sexuality has been suddenly recognized . . . the interpretation of dreams confirmed . . . and the necessity of psychoanalytic therapy of hysteria carried . . . in Parliament. I have obviously become reputable again . . ."

Ernest Jones devotes only a few paragraphs to the winning of the appointment and erroneously credits it to the gift of the Böcklin.

One of the considerations compelling belief that Stone's material is far more factual than fictional, is his obvious lack of creative ability. This subjective factor determined his writing career for his best selling biographical novels were compiled from research about celebrities he had never met. As an investigator and compiler, Stone is thorough and hard working. Though he does dramatize his research to secure interest, his lack of imagination compels him to be factual. Consequently he dramatizes what is really dramatical.

As has been so often mentioned, one of the greatest crises in Freud's life was his discovery that tales of sexual molestation by their parents were but the fantasies of his patients which he had accepted at face value. To assuage his chagrin, he consoled himself that believing these fantasies was not so very fatal, for fantasies could be as powerful as realities and should be dealt with on the same level. He had been told by Bernheim (incidentally, Stone's chapter on Freud's visit to Bernheim is about the best in his book) that we are all "hallucinating creatures." Bernheim had also supplied the technique for dispelling such hallucinations — simple, direct and effective suggestion with or without accompanying hypnosis — which Freud chose to discard for the free association of ideas.

Characteristically, Freud did not admit he was taken in by the seduction fantasies until eight years later, but the damage to his ego and to his fortunes can be guessed from his admission that reality had been lost and he would have been glad to give up his quest for the neurotic grail but had no idea of where to turn.

Stone supplies the pertinent details to this crisis in Freud's career with great clarity despite his saccharinity. It happened in 1897, shortly after Freud returned from a vacation and he had written the most remarkable of all his letters, renouncing his *neurotica,* demolishing the credibility of unconscious outpourings which had no "indication of reality" indistinguishable from "emotional charged fiction." (Quotation marks are Stone's. Actually they are the exact phrases Freud used in his letters to Fliess, but Stone gives no intimation of this source).

In Stone's account, Freud was compelled to admit his gullibility because a woman patient began doubting the fantasy of her father's molestation.

"I have been misled," Stone has him saying to himself. "We are not dealing here with child molestation. We are dealing with *fantasy!* With what, in their earliest childhood, these patients *wished for.*"

Freud was so disconcerted, that after dismissing the woman he also cancelled his appointment with his last patient of the day, and excused himself from the evening meal to go for a long walk. During his walk, a scene which had kept recurring at the rim of consciousness since he was seven, which had often been consciously revived and repeated in manifold forms in his dreams, again clamored for interpretation. Yet he had never attempted to form any conclusions about his actions and motives in that scene when he had invaded his parents' bedroom when they were supposedly asleep with the door firmly closed, though not locked.

Stone followed with a rhapsody about Freud's agonized self-searching to understand himself. Oh, the power of words to hide the truth, a power which Freud knew so well! One of the most monstrous acts of disrespect, sheer brutishness and incredible gall becomes glibly translated into a noble desire to search for the truth of all human motivation. This was Freud's own primal scene, far outside the norm. In the entire history of civilization, its occurrence must be extremely rare, dismissed as insane or the completely bestial act of a monster.

Through this traumatic episode, Freud's subsequent actions and motivations can be reconstructed. The emotional effects of Freud's perverse deed haunted him throughout his life, for he admitted that his father's angry remark spurred him on to continuing achievement, "as if to say, you see I have amounted to something after all."

His incredible act was a natural consequence of the undue favoritism of his mother, which he had hallucinated into a sexual relationship. The generation gap between his father and mother was no more than the age gap between him and his mother. Their marriage was illicit and incestuous to him, yet sanctioned by society. It is understandable why he had no respect whatsoever for the sanctity of privacy, marriage, authority, rules, professional ethics or social taboos or customs because he could not respect his parents' marriage.

On the other hand, Freud could also have been terribly uncertain whether the scene was real or only an hallucination, or purely somnambulistic. No wonder he accepted fantasies as realities for so long, troubled as he could have been by his uncertainty whether his own primal scene was real or imagined. His willingness to believe the fantasies of sexual molestation by parents, which was even more criminal than his childish attempt at mother incest, becomes quite understandable.

Stone evidently did not realize the significance of his revelation. As has been disclosed, Freud published the urinating incident in his dreamology without the details that Stone supplies which clarifies the episode so dramatically. It accounts for Freud's personality development and subsequent trend of thought, so completely and thoroughly that detailed discussion is hardly necessary.

It is however worth learning why Jones and other biographers mentioning this urinating incident, did not find the facts Stone uncovered. Other biographers merely repeat Freud's statement that he deliberately urinated in his parents' bedroom. They fail to sense the rage and anger which must have stirred his father to growl he "would never amount to anything," a remark he knew would hurt the most, in view of Sigmund's inordinate ambition.

The failure of other biographers to discover the material Stone unearthed may be because it was very carefully hidden by Freud. It may also be possible that his boast that he had destroyed his confidential notes was another lie. If preserved, eventually thay were collected into the archives but never made accessible or were overlooked in the mass of his writings until Stone dug them up.

Curious about the source of this spectacular information I wrote Stone and asked him to indicate whether he had secured it from diaries, memoranda, or unpublished papers resting in the London archives. He was kind enough to reply that the information was published in Freud's *Collected Works* as part of his self analysis! Regretting his inability to supply the exact reference as the index was incomplete because of the translator's death, he suggested that I wade through all twenty-one of the volumes to dig it out.

Though incredulous that such a damaging revelation

would be available in his writings, I went through the index carefully reading every reference to Freud's mother and father and to the primal scene but failed to find any such material.

Consequently, I became suspicious that Stone was either pulling my leg or that he had not written the primal scene material himself but had delegated it to one of his assistants. It is commonly known that a writer who is very successful hires lesser writers to do his research, if not much of his writing. Consequently Stone had only a vague knowledge of the subject which was betrayed in his TV interview.

At any rate, it was rewarding just to scan Freud's immense production of words in those twenty-one volumes. Reading him, gives one an awesome impression of his hypermanic thinking which gave him no rest and impelled him to such prodigious feats of composition. In that scanning, I ran across his reference to his credulity in accepting the seduction phantasies of his female patients which he alibied was a justifiable error and not greatly to his discredit.

## CHAPTER 10

# Freudian Time

*"One might ask me whether and how far I am convinced of the correctness of the assumptions here developed. My answer would read that I am neither myself convinced nor do I ask that others shall believe them; or better stated, I don't know how far I believe them."*

This pose of skepticism, was a mockery in view of Freud's fanatic insistence that his sexual dogma must become an "unshakeable bulwark."[1] This was another swing, to a tepid renunciation of his *neurotica*. These swings prevailed throughout Freud's life, though they were less violent in his old age.

Otherwise, time left little trace upon him; his face remained remarkably childlike and immature even into his sixties. His emotions were fixed by the double trauma of his primal scene. He was both terrified by his father's angry outburst, "That boy will never amount to anything," and enraptured by his mother's tender caresses when she carried him back to bed. He was her true love; his father the interloper, he assuaged himself.

Freud was subjected to many shocks during his tempestuous life, and often rudely jolted by the unpleasant and terrifying. But he also was thrilled by the praise and love showered upon him. This, too, can be traumatic. Suddenly coming into a huge fortune, making a great discovery, writing a best seller or attaining instant fame, can unbalance a person as badly as a sudden catastrophe. Both extremes of emotion are hard to accommodate to the nervous system.

Freud's tenacity in clinging to his incestual longings may indicate how rapturously he responded to what he thought were his mother's sexual advances which favored him over his father. Favoring a child over a grown man excites monumental conceit and also gives rise to feeling omnipotent. Dissolving his incestual fixation would also dissolve his feeling of omnipotence, or "authority" as Freud termed it to Jung.

Trauma alters time perception; the inner clock slows down when severely jarred. A painful jolt leaves in its wake a terror of repetition. On the other hand, ecstasy demands repetition; when only misery results, the consequences are sad.

Freud's painful alienation from Fliess was compounded by his desperate circumstances. His time perception altered; patients once quickly relieved of their suffering to spare their funds, were gradually induced to return for more and more visits in the manner already elucidated. Eventually analyses became "interminable," as if he could not cure.

This contradicts the established laws of learning for every art or skill acquired reduces performance time. But Freud did not suspend the laws of learning because from his standpoint, he progressed from not knowing how to hold patients to knowing how to bind them to him as long as he pleased.

The practical advantages of no time limits are obvious. An analyst renting out his couch to 100 patients for ten hours each or 10 patients for 100 hours receives the same income, but it is certainly more advantageous to limit patients and extend hours. When the turn over is big, much time is lost. Besides, spreading analyses too widely dispels the glamour because it becomes too easy to get. Every detriment of psychoanalysis as a science or therapy became an advantage from a purely financial standpoint.

When a patient was dismissed, the psychic hold upon

him persisted. As Freud told Alexander, the transference continues even if the patient never sees his analyst again. This prevents any retrospective appraisal free of transference influences which would enable a patient to review his analysis realistically.

Analysts needed only a few patients in their hey day Suppose one demanded a minimum of three years with four or five visits weekly. He need book only about eight patients and gradually replace them to stay in practice. Some patients would not last the three years; others would find the couch comfortable for five, ten or even more years. If the analyst retired after twenty years or so, his entire career would have been limited to about sixty or seventy patients.

Theoretically his entire career could be confined to only one patient if one was rich enough to afford full time. Of course, that is only a mathematical possibility; in reality it would be highly improbable. A man with limitless funds would have limitless choices and probably tire of the same analyst.

Theodore Reik, perhaps the most obnoxious, blatant and pestiferous of Freudians, almost landed just such a fish. Reik was persuaded by Freud to become a lay analyst and he never tired of reminding the world of his distinction. Even the Freudians loathed him and denied him entree to their society which forced him to form his own.

Once when reclining on the Couch of Couches, Reik absentmindedly jingled some coins in his pocket. This slight act was of deep psychological import, Reik ventured to say, symptomatic of his anal-erotic tendencies. Though an orthodox interpretation the Great One was irritated by his temerity in voicing an opinion of his own, and snorted:

"That is, of course, nonsense. You think of your brothers and are glad you are now able to send them money."

Obediently Reik scanned his thoughts and did discover some fleeting impression which confirmed Freud's interpretation.

To get back to the point of an exclusive retainer, Reik

was once so favored by an eccentric millionaire. The man was almost insane however and appeared for only two seances in three months. Reik felt guilty about this and dismissed him. Freud laughed over the matter and advised him to form a "sclerotic conscience."

The clock never moved with Reik either. He was one of the Viennese who opposed Jung's tenure during his stormy affiliation. In a posthumous publication of his reminiscenses sponsored by his disciples[2] Reik was quoted as objecting to Jung because he "was too goyish."

When pressed to clarify what he meant by "too goyish," Reik replied:

"Oh, he talked very loud and very decisive, authoritative. He was blond and tall. I think he (Freud) was attracted to him originally because Freud was small and Jewish-looking, don't forget. . . . Jung was prejudiced against Jews. It was not correct that he gave it up when he came to Freud. Jung was the son of a pastor and that had an influence upon his teaching. He did not give up his anti-Semitism."

Time has had little effect upon the Freudian mind, as Reik's animadversions illustrate, nor has it had much effect on the dogma, as rigid and unchangeable as any religion.The Bible's message is still the same; new versions have merely changed the phrasing. Believers have diminished in number but many are still devout. Freud too is becoming passé, but his dogma still endures because only a few patients can support an analyst. Its very expense gives it status because comparatively few can afford it.

Great expense connotes great quality. Though this is true of diamonds, motor cars, mansions and other status symbols, it is not at all true of psychoanalysis. The more paid for it, the less it is worth. When patients can afford only one or two weekly visits, and analysts now accept them for they must to survive, the hold upon them is much looser. There is more time for reflection between seances and with reflection comes disillusionment.

Recent indications continue to show a steady decline in Freudian fortunes. Their monopoly has been broken; various independent movements, catering to the desire for quicker and less expensive procedures, have found support. The Jung, Adler and Rank schools have been incremented by other Freudian offshoots, the Horneyites, the William A. White School and Harry Stack Sullivan's. More recently, Glasser's "Reality Therapy," has prospered. He, too, once practiced psychoanalysis.

Perhaps the most consistently successful psychotherapist today is Joseph Wolpe who has developed conditioning therapies based on the work of Pavlov, to a high degree of effectiveness. Dr. Wolpe was also once a Freudian and has suffered from their usual vindictiveness. His method is based on getting the patient to re-experience his original trauma under simulated conditions which gradually extinguishes their effects.

Actually, is that not what all psychiatrists may be trying to do? In their offices, they try to get the patient to relate his difficulties, which means reliving them. If the psychiatrist is understanding and provides some insight into the mechanisms which perpetuate the undesired behavior or reactions, they are re-conditioning the patient. According to Wolpe:

> "Neurotic habits are distinguished by their resistance to extinction in the face of their unadaptiveness."

Emulating Freud, psychoanalysts continually disparage therapies that show promise and effectiveness. At first they were amused by Wolpe's "naive," "superficial" and "mechanistic" procedures, predicting quick relapses. When these did not occur, they extended the time and predicted relapses would be inevitable. When after seven years of follow ups, these relapses still had not come about, the analysts labeled them "transference cures" or mere "ego strengthening" for "fortuitous sampling."

Still others attributed the results to Wolpe's "therapeutic personality" but this was contradicted by the fact that the same results were obtained by therapists with widely diverging personalities. When the conditioning therapies could no longer be denied, the analysts grudgingly accepted them for only a limited range and ascribed this effectiveness to "psychoanalytic" mechanisms.

The current vogue of *I'm O.K., You're O.K.* by Dr. Thomas A. Harris, indicates a further flight from the couch, accelerated by dissatisfaction with the slow, cumbersome and frustrating Freudian approach. Harris' "O.K." method is based on the school of Berne and Harry Stack Sullivan, another split from Freudianetics known as "transactional analysis." It has a very sound neurological basis, and relies on neurological research which has established that the brain is a highly sensitive recording instrument and retains sensations from birth. These sensations, emotions and impulses originating before the faculty of speech or thought was developed, account for the retention of infantile characteristics long into maturity. It is a far more thorough and logical development of Rank's "birth trauma" theory and suggests that our unconscious thinking and feeling originated before consciousness was fully developed.

It is interesting to regard these new approaches, now being promulgated directly to the public. It is reminiscent of the appeal that Freud once exerted and is still quite strong. When Freudian enthusiasts are seen in a large group as I had occasion several years ago in attending Freudian sponsored lectures,the giddy atmosphere was somewhat sickening. The chief speaker was a remarkably cool and detached high priest, completely unaffected by the rapturous throbs of his audience.

Another speaker was a young Ph.D., who expounded on the nobility of Freud's character and the anti-Semitism he had suffered. In dwelling on the old, oft repeated story of how his father's hat was tossed into the street by a vicious anti-Semite, he seemed oblivious to the fact that Freud showed little sympathy for his father's humiliation.

The hands of the Freudian clock move but slowly. Despite Freud's immense literary production, the paucity of his ideas is amazing. Like advertising slogans, they are repeated over and over again. Once I met a man who told me he had heard Freud when he was a guest at a London

hotel, waiting for his last home to be prepared. His remarks to his fellow guests in the lobby were straight out of
"The Psychopathology of Everyday Life," on the errors of
typesetters which he suggested were unconsciously motivated.

Belief in Freud himself can remain fixed and unchanged, even in those who have departed from his movement. In the fifties, I once attended a golf outing sponsored
by physicians. One very courteously invited me to join
him. He was an athletically built fellow and to my surprise, a psychoanalyst. He was also a whale of a golfer,
something of a hustler I suspected, for his score of seventy
was the sensation of the day as was his loot in prizes.

We became friendly during our round and he professed
some interest in seeing my manuscript which I warned
him was hostile. Several weeks later when we discussed it
over the phone, he objected to my labeling Freud a charlatan because of my experiences with his disciples.

"They were only following his charlatanry," I told him.

He literally gasped. In a tone trembling with fear and
anxiety, he terminated our conversation.

Later I learned he was one of Franz Alexander's fair
haired boys and had re-located with him in California.
Several months ago, I decided to phone him. He remembered me well and was quick to tell me he had severed
connections with psychoanalysis.

He saw me between patients. During the intervening
eighteen years he had become the typical mod in dress and
language which reeked with profanity. He called my attention to a framed placard reading:

"Never mind the bull shit."

Then he recited the harrowing story of his traumatic
separation from Alexander and psychoanalysis because of
his heresies. He had won a generous reserch grant but
when he presented his independent views before the brethren, all hell broke loose. One fanatic rose from his seat,
approached the lecture platform and bellowed:

"This is not psychoanalysis."

He cursed his former Freudian associates, bitterly and

profanely. Curiously enough, he still regarded Freud as a great thinker. As he continued talking, his conversation took a maudlin, incoherent tone and he too presented a distressing picture of the havoc psychoanalysis can work upon its practitioners. His trusting belief in Freud proved he had learned but little since our first conversation, and except for his rancor, his attitude was practically unchanged. He had retreated into some branch of psychiatry such as marriage counselling but he showed very little therapeutic enthusiasm or interest.

Freudian time does march on, slow though their clock may be. The constant preoccupation with Freud's personality has culminated in the most remarkable expose of all — *Brother Animal*.[3] To collect his findings, Roazen spent many years of interviewing everyone available who had had some contact with Freud to solve the mystery of his relationship with Tausk.

On the basis of Roazen's findings, it would seem that Freud grew progressively demented with the years. His death wish phantasmagoria tricked him into believing even his closest associates were casting an evil eye upon him. Of Fedner whose loyalty to him was really touching, he once told Alexander:

"I can't stand the parricidal look in his eyes."

If he believed his own death wishes had killed his infant brother, then he could also believe death wishes could kill him. Freud believed Jung had harbored a death wish and eventually anyone who could pose a threat to his prestige, became objects of his death wishes in self defense. Freud's animosity to Tausk, an unquestionable factor in his suicide, was aroused by intense rivalry. Tausk removed his rivalry by his suicide.

He was a tall, handsome man but also a bit erratic for he had abandoned journalism for law and law for psychoanalysis. He served capably as an officer during World War I and though a somewhat glamorous figure because of his many love affairs, he was also contentious and at times, unpleasant.

Lou Andreas-Salome had been his mistress. Freud also

had a yen for her but proclaimed it was non-sexual. His inhibitions probably made coitus impossible, which also probably aggravated his jealousy of Tausk who was far from inhibited sexually. Freud could have feared Tausk both for his intellectual capacities and his romantic accomplishments. When Tausk implored him for analysis Freud refused, possibly fearing his own sexual inexperience would become exposed during their intimacy.

With typical cunning, Freud arranged for Tausk's analysis with Helene Deutsch who was then undergoing analysis with him. Through her, Freud could probe Tausk's psyche without risk to himself. Through Deutsch he may have managed to plant the ideas that eventually impelled Tausk to suicide. As Oberndorf reported, Freud believed he was not obligated to prevent suicide.

When Tausk ended his life, Freud showed little concern. He was equally indifferent to the suicide of Silberer, another adulant who had pined for his couch, several months after Freud brutally rejected him. Freud's remarkable hypnotic powers probably had some diabolic influence in causing these suicides. In "Analysis Terminable and Interminable" Freud admitted: "When a man is endowed with power it is hard for him not to misuse it."

Roazen's study is replete with such intimate tidbits as: Freud once fell asleep with a lighted cigar during a seance with Deutsch and was awakened by the odor of his burning carpet. Freud psychoanalyzed his daughter Anna. (No doubt he found it easy to confirm his Oedipal theories with her). One son pursued an affair with one of his patients; none of his three sons were interested in analysis as a career which disappointed Freud greatly. (That may account for him calling Anna his son). Freud was considered "garrulous" by some friends. He once tried to dissuade a young relative from over coddling her child.

However, the most damaging revelation concerned his diagnostic incompetence, for he could not distinguish between neuroses and psychoses, as Roazen's findings would indicate:

"Freud sometimes treated cases psychoanalytically, as if they were neurotics when it later turned out that much more serious trouble underlay a mere façade of neurosis. Freud saw psychotics as patients without realizing the severity of their illness. For example, he sometimes cured a neurotic symptom, only for the patient to fall back on an underlying psychosis. In one case where the original symptoms had been agoraphobia (fear of open spaces) Freud had to reintroduce the agoraphobia through hypnosis in order to undo the damage of the treatment."

"As Freud once wrote to a distressed pupil 'you have had the bad luck to run into a latent paranoia, and through the cure of his neurosis, you may have freed the way for a more serious illness. That happens to each of us occasionally and there is no protection against it."⁴

That reasoning sounds insane, equivalent to saying that curing a cold only brought on pneumonia. But who was there to challenge this omniscient man's opinions? He was a law unto himself, his authority autonomous, for psychoanalysis has never submitted to outside regulation. Though members of the American Psychiatric Association, Freudians hold their own meetings at the site of the APA convention a few days before the general assembly and depart before it starts.

Freud's miraculous influence became exercised through his clever capitalization of his theory of unconscious thinking and feeling, using the analogy of the iceberg (as his teacher Lipps had before him) to draw a thoroughly meretricious comparison. He overrode objections to his interpretations on the grounds they were dictated by unconscious factors.

The fraudulence is obvious. Though unconscious thoughts could be due to repression as he claimed, there is also the possibility that the unconscious thoughts he insinuated were present, never really had existed. By attributing any reluctance to accept his interpretations to "resistance" Freud forced his Oedipal obsessions upon the world as a psychological discovery.

We can be just as unaware of unconscious thought due to repression as we could if they never had occurred. For example, a literary critic, probably Brandes, once told Freud he accepted all his theories except for mother incest, as he had never been aware of such longings.

"But it need not have been conscious," Freud glibly asserted and claimed the critic accepted this interpretation. Whether the man really believed Freud or tactfully declined to argue the matter is of course impossible to prove, but the one likelihood is just as possible as the other. A patient in the throes of transference would no doubt believe implicitly. Actually, Freud used coercion, as the coin jingling interpretation Reik was black jacked into accepting would prove.

Upon such thoroughly irrelevant, trivial and useless interpretations, Freud built his reputation for miraculous insight. The goal of psychoanalysis is the interpretation, nothing else really matters. Interpreting was a delight to Freud; he reveled in displaying his intellectual virtuosity. As he lamented to Fliess, "It's a pity one cannot make a living by dream interpretation alone."

How his patients fared, whether or not his interpretations helped, simply did not concern him.

"It was against my will that I had to concern myself with therapy," he confessed, but all indications are that his concern was slight.

## CHAPTER 11

# The Dogma Applied

*"It sounds unpleasant and it is still more paradoxical but it must nevertheless be said that whoever would really be free and therefore happy in the love-life must give up respect for women and adapt himself to the idea of incest with mother and sister."*

Written at fifty-two, this pronunciamento proclaims that of all women, no matter how tempting and voluptuous, women whom society for the most part sanctions intimacy, the only ones man really lusts for are his closest relatives, the very ones whom society forbids entertaining carnal thoughts.

This is perversity on a pathological level yet this teaching is being followed and applied under the delusion it was the inspiration of a genius. Moreover, it was advocated in the name of freedom and "happiness in the love life." Actually Freud was merely expressing his own innate desires and saying:

"In order to be happy in my love life, I had to adapt myself to the idea of incest and abjure all other forms of love."

Reading current psychoanalytic literature will reveal how this ghastly idea is applied, with the end of casting all mankind in the role of Sigmund Freud. "Being in Love and Object Loss,"[1] delivered April 13, 1971 as the twenty-first Freud lecture is a prime example of this distorted thinking:

"Freud hinted at the considerable role that narcissistic women play in man's love life. He saw this as
man's attempt to regain his lost narcissism through
the object. There is an attraction between these cold,
narcissistic power driven women with overwhelming
penis envy and men who are atoning Oedipal guilt
throughout their lives. The fact that (Maugham's) *Of
Human Bondage* and Heinrich Mann's Professor
Anrath(made into the film "The Blue Angel,") had
such a wide appeal is because they depict a universal
danger: Self annihilation through love."

These sweeping interpretations are typical Freud.
Since he was attracted by a "narcissistic" woman, as he
regarded Lou Andreas-Salome, all mankind follows suit to
atone for their Oedipal guilt. As for the wide appeal of "The
Blue Angel," Marlene Dietrich's singing of "Falling in
Love Again," and Emil Janning's superb portrayal of a
lonely teacher, susceptible to the wiles of a floosy, is commonly attributed to the success of this remarkable film,
not self annihilation through love.

This paper was delivered by a physician high in standing, collecting considerable fees for his services. Just how
beneficial his services were he revealed in another paper.[2]
His patient was highly competent in his profession but had
no social life. His homosexuality, according to this analyst
his third, was confined to "inconspicuous touches."

As the previous two analyses had produced "no appreciable transference" the author confessed reluctance about
trying a third but succumbed to the plea of the second, a
"very competent, warm and direct woman, we cannot
abandon him."

Four years later, when "the therapeutic result was
practically nil" the third analysis grinded to a halt, worthless either as a therapy or as an investigation, the author
confessed, a wasting of "the patient's money." (Four years
of analysis consumes about 800 hours on the couch). "This
should not happen," the author lamented and asked his
audience, assembled at their annual meeting of 1969, "I

wonder how many such cases are remembered?"

Acknowledging that the patient should have been rejected "after a few months of trial", he recommended trial
analyses which would permit deciding after "a year or so
whether the analysis would be productive enough to war-
rant continuation."

A careful examination of this author's statements
leads to the conclusion that he was echoing everything
Freud had written in his remarkable "Analysis, Terminable and Interminable," which alibied very eloquently for
the unpredictable vagaries of his method. Actually, the
rambling, incoherent flow of free associations could be
blamed for indeterminate and inconclusive, or "interminable" as Freud termed it, analyses.

At any rate, the author's frankness in admitting that
trial analyses are unpredictable was quite unusual. He
also reminded his audience:

"Major psychoanalytic institutes discontinue
training of about twenty-five per cent of candidates
after thorough admission procedures and/or clinical
investigations; we can hardly be smug about our pre-
dictive capacity."

He further reminded his colleagues (but were they
listening?) that failures account for analyses of ten years
and more, without "appreciable results" until the procedure "degenerates into supportive therapy." This, too, follows the "Analysis, Terminable and Interminable" line,
for Freud sanctioned such failures as he believed a complete analysis was impossible and some patients would
need the couch all their lives.

The author blamed these failures on the brevity of
training analyses. Of 918, 107 lasted "only" 300 to 400
hours; only 51 had 900 to 1,000 hours of couch time; the
remaining 760 having from 400 to 900 hours. Longer
training analyses, however, could be blamed for the
failure in treatment, prolonged because the analyst
needed to recoup the heavy expense of his own training. So
much for this author, a confessed disciple of Ferenczi
which could account for his unusual concern for therapeu-

tic results.    In the same issue, appeared this gobbledegook:

    ". . . libidinal aggressive object cathexes of the
    Oedipus complex by repression are kept in a deficient
    mode of discharge process with objects; they are not
    'destroyed' and assimilated by the coherent ego but
    are instead repressed, i.e., maintained in a state of
    lower psychic organization and interaction with ob-
    jects continue to take place on lower levels of psychic
    organization."

Another author on the *menschenkenner* theme:

    "I would like to repeat that we would be well
    advised to continue to listen to and, if necessary,
    revaluate the insistence of children, assorted infan-
    tile grown-ups and creative writers that we know
    better for they have given to psychoanalysis some of
    its most constructive insights. However, no one is
    infallible and the creative writer or psychoanalyst
    has no more claim to infallibility than Popes, chil-
    dren, dogs or schizophrenics."

Another paper introduced "Psychological Mindedness"
into the terminology, defining it as "a person's ability to
see relationships among thoughts, feelings and actions
with the goal of learning meanings and causes of his experience and behavior." The classic "Analysis, Terminable
and Interminable" was cited as having established three
factors determining success or failure: Strength of instinct, severity of early trauma and capacity for ego modification, defined as "the degree of propensity for
psychosis."

But Freud often failed to detect psychoses, although
there is always the possibility that the neuroses he treated
degenerated into psychoses through following the wholly
irrational free association of ideas. Franz Alexander too
confessed his inability to predict whether or not analyses
would be comparatively simple and brief or long and complicated.

To a cynic, the inability of the Freudians to select
suitable patients would seem to originate from their

method of selection. Only those capable of paying for their long, fruitless and expensive procedures are accepted; all other considerations are secondary.

As for "Psychological mindedness", it would seem to be just another term for "insight," but an authority quoted in this paper, believed it embraced several "ego functions . . . influenced by factors from all psychic structures but particularly by the existence of a well developed superego since it is this structure which represents compliance with the injunction to be candid, to see, communicate and think about all experiences in behavior in the interest of cooperation with the analytic and therapeutic intention."

Interestingly enough, free associations once hailed as an immortal discovery is not mentioned, which may indicate that new terms are being introduced because the old ones have become stale and meaningless.

This issue of the *International Journal* yielded the case history of a woman who complained she could not remember, concentrate nor understand her husband's business. As her IQ scores were judged below her true ability, the author contended that her taboo against "seeing" dated from when she slept in her parents' bedroom and repeatedly witnessed the primal scene. This was one of Freud's favorite interpretations. When he inferred from Marie Bonaparte's dream material that she had once witnessed a carnal scene staged by a groom and maid in her family's retinue, it won her lifelong allegiance.

Another paper, "Establishment and Disruption of the Psychoanalytic Modus Vivendi," is a daring departure; Freud is not cited. Jazzing up the terminology is of course commendable; one must admit that "modus vivendi" at least has style but it merely means establishing transference, by "creating a climate in which the patient can regress, to induce the patien to make his analyst the object of his repressed wishes and the various motives he has of avoiding experiencing his wishes."

Almost every paper betrays a continuing stagnation and use of foolish reasoning. Reports of a successful case are absent; at least the journals consulted contained no such reports. Failure and prolonged frustration seem the essence of psychoanalytic experience, the same failure which Freud disguised as success in his ghastly "Analysis Terminable and Interminable."

For example, he maintained that though patients had undergone beneficial analyses, sometime "new events" provoked new pathology which justified returning to the couch again. In a symposium (we are still on the same issue) one contributor was in the middle of his third year with a patient who had undergone just such a "successful" analysis four years before her marriage. Her "new event" was the neglect of her husband after the birth of a son.

In the hour reported, she withdrew into a silence and "half reverie" which the analyst confessed he found annoying. On rising to leave, she broke her silence by commenting on his flowers. In "calm, poised" tones, evidently to hide his emotion, he told her they were called "Peace," whereupon she burst into laughter and left smiling. Interpretation:

"The patient's sadomasochistic rage was a narcissistic transference resistance which induced in the analyst a parallel defensive process of futility, anger and somnolence."

Another of his patients also burst into laughter when her pottie reminiscences were associated with a desire for regularity, which re-established a faltering rapport. Another patient, middle aged and widowed by her husband's suicide was in a transference tinged with eroticism, which also depressed the analyst into somnolence. He felt her case, only a few months along, was hopeless.

"You have been disappointed by men — now I will disappoint you," he glumly predicted. The effect was startling; the woman's tone changed, and collaboration ensued. The analyst's mood also lifted to bring a corresponding lift to the patient.

The effects of suggestion are ignored in psychoanalysis, but these three little vignettes were the only indications of benefit or buoyancy in all the papers discussed.

*The Psychoanalytic Quarterly, #2*, 1973, yields several

items of interest. Smiley Blanton's book[3] about his analysis with Freud, one of his very last, was reviewed. Because Freud had been rescued from the Nazi's through American help, Blanton asked him if he then thought better of Americans.

"No," said the great *menschenkenner.*

The reviewer of an anti-Freudian book, *Science and Psychoanalysis,* provoked because Freud's dream theories were labeled therein as aberrational, wondered sourly that if the authors "differ so widely and so fundamentally from Freud, why are they not equally emboldened to change the name of the discipline under which they operate?"

This is another echo from Freud who did assert very emphatically during his troubles with Jung and other dissidents, that only he knew what psychoanalysis was all about, and therefore it should be identified solely with his name.[4]

The same issue announced publication of the Menninger report on psychoanalytic therapy,[5] compiled from a project begun in 1954, based on only forty-two patients.

In 1919, G. Stanley Hall had boasted oy "thousands" of Freudian cures, but thirty years later Oberndorf could not establish any therapeutic standards with his colleagues, nor induce them to submit cases in analysis for a year or more before a board to review the advisability of continuing.

Another case study[6] displayed the urgent need for such consultations. The patient discussed, age fifty-five, had seen more than 25 analysts in forty years, most only once or twice, but about ten up to six months; five up to a year, one for two years, another three years and still another, four years, logging in all over 1,700 hours. The patient was described as quarrelsome and foul smelling whose odor lingered for several hours.

This journal also reported a new wrinkle — reading body movements to correlate them with emerging themes. The author believed he could predict the appearance of oral fantasies by the flexion of an already crossed leg and

that study of such non-verbal behavior had brought forth a
highly sophisticated science. He cited no references.

Reading body movements implies resorting to a sign
language. The ability to talk is man's sole possession;
reading body movements may be a form of regression into
the dark past before language was developed. The
monotonous drone of free associations may account for this
new ploy. To fight off somnolence, analysts may have to
force themselves to keep their eyes wide open, watching
the patient rather than listening to him. The analyst can
also analyze his own body movements to keep himself
occupied, which yielded this material:     A patient with
three years on the couch was depressed because her boy
friend had been very late in calling at her apartment,
would not stay the night and had left abruptly. When she
mentioned the possibility of leaving for a short vacation
and missing several hours, the analyst touched his wed-
ding ring, which he interpreted as expressing "in a way,"
that he understood her mood. Though it could have been a
request to wave the rule of guaranteeing appointments so
she could have the money for a short vacation, the
analyst's preoccupation with his own body movement exposes a possible new form of exploitation: Not only do
patients endow Freudian researches, they may also be
financing the analyst's self analysis of his own body
movements.

Another patient's stiff rigidity and tenseness was attributed to fear of his homosexual passivity, as if warding
off attack. On the couch he was silent, unyielding and
unable to relax for many hours at great expense before the
ice was broken. His "latent homosexuality" so freely diagnosed upon such insubstantial grounds, was consequently
exploited whereas a few suggestions to relax could have
saved much time and expense.

Freud's shadow looms over every contribution. The
same issue printed three of his letters squabbling with
Andre Breton, founder of surrealism. Freud's rancor rose
because Breton inquired why reference to an author of a
work on symbolism was omitted from later editions of his

dreamology. Quite distraught, Freud admitted he was sensitive to criticism, claimed that the unbounded ambition of his childhood had been overcome and blamed Otto Rank for deleting the reference from later editions. It is very possible that he lied and had ordered the deletion, just as he had lied so shamelessly to Fliess in denying leaking his material to Weininger.

Still, the Freudian clock does move, if ever so slowly for "All Roads Lead to Rome," reveals a startling development — discussion of Freud's own Oedipality. His long standing reluctance to visit the Holy City, eventually surmounted, was connected with Freud's reticence about his mother. "All Roads Lead to Rome," consequently became "All Interpretations Lead to the Oedipus Complex," for the author interpreted Freud's fear of visiting Rome as "the result of incestuous wishes toward his mother and the specific choice of the city an unconscious representation of his feelings toward his Catholic nursemaid at two and a half."

The nursemaid's many appearances in Freud's dreams was interpreted as mother substitution so the path of interpretation ran thusly:

Catholic nursemaid-mother substitute-Oedipus complex-fear of visiting Rome. In the mania for applying the Oedipal dogma, many valid constructions are missed. It is true, the nursemaid could have had a very important influence on Freud's life. She had been very fond of him and predicted he would some day be great. She took him to Mass many times and also coaxed him to show her the family hoard. Then she suddenly disappeared and little Sigmund later learned she had been jailed for stealing the gold coins he had shown her.

Introducing little Sigmund to the impressive Catholic rituals may account for his aversion to the Jewish religion, overawed by the power and prestige of Catholicism. Psychoanalysis and Catholicism show many similarities. Both are basically power structures. Both the confessional and the couch dispense absolution at a price. Both have sexual foundations, the Immaculate Conception and the

Oedipus Complex. Sigmund Freud like the Pope, ordained his cardinals from behind his couch. His hesitancy in visiting Rome was overcome after he became famous and his awe may have diminished.

Another bizarre feature of psychoanalysis is the entrapment of men such as Oberndorf who are really dissidents but cannot sever the psychic bonds imprisoning them. One such penetrating, skeptic is Allen Wheelis of San Francisco who is also gifted with remarkable literary talent. A reading of any of his works leaves one wondering how he can cling to the dogma but he does. His thinly disguised autobiography, *The Quest for Identity*[7] contains a chapter, "The Vocational Hazards of Psychoanalysis" which is more devastating than anything the most hostile opponent could compose.

Wheelis admits that some form of lethargy overtakes an analyst because the money comes so easy. Of the diversity of interpretation, he has observed:

"A dozen psychoanalysts listening to the same material are likely to formulate a dozen different estimations of unconscious meaning, of its prognostic significance and of the specific interpretation which should be made."[8]

This diversity did not faze French, co-author with Franz Alexander on therapy. He has averred that different interpretations of the same dream can all be correct. French was Coyne Campbell's training analyst. His transference with French was decidedly negative and was expressed to me in down-to-earth language, expressive of his intense aversion.

"Primacy of Genitality in the Light of Ego Psychology,"[10] reveals a refreshing independence of mind by challenging one of Freud's most hoary tenets — complete sexual potency precludes the existence of a neurosis. (The reader may recall that he got this notion when a nervous patient he confined to a sanitarium enjoyed the embraces of a pretty co-resident every night and was cured.)

Contrary to the primacy of genitality theory, the author reported the case of a neurotic woman who nevertheless functioned very well sexually despite an inadequate husband. The author's "control analyst" (supervisor of beginning analysts) could not explain this contradiction. The author also presented the case of a mature, well balanced woman whose sex life was "poor compared to his neurotic case."

Such cases expose again the dangerous diagnostic incompetence of Freud which his disciples imitate. They regard inadequate sexuality as a form of neurosis requiring years of encouchment which itself may induce a neurosis where none existed before. The author did not so state, but the implication is unmistakeable. He did conclude:

"The variations and combinations of genital and personality functioning range along a spectrum which defies classification . . . it should occasion no surprise that the theory of genital primacy is now being challenged in the light of observations made by analysts for many years."

However, such observations seldom appear in print. Voicing them privately "for many years," reveals the conspirational motif in suppressing valid data which could compel a complete invalidation of all Freud's tenets. Suppression of such observations constitutes malpractice, as flagrant as pursuing research under the guise of therapy. The final irony is the suppression of the results of this unsanctioned research because it conflicts with theory. The critic of the genitality supremacy theory then asked his colleagues this extremely pertinent question:

"To what extent do the limitations of analysts' own orgiastic capacities influence the achievement of genital primacy in their patients?"

There are now increasing reports that analysts test their orgiastic capacities on their own couches and their experiments are charged on their bills. Several years ago, a woman sued her analyst in Los Angeles because she was billed for coitus. Intimacies with patients are becoming more and more prevalent, even among psychologists and some ugly squabbles have been aired. Recently an "advice

to the lovelorn" columnist published a woman's complaint
that her physician, an internist, had enjoyed her favors
after office hours and then had the gall to bill her, though
no medical services were rendered. She was advised:

"A fee? He should be booted out of the medical
profession. And if you really want to shake the old
boy up, tell him you're a professional and send him a
bill."

A deep note of disillusionment and rebellion is vividly
expressed in "Psychoanalysis and American
Psychology,"[12] by Ernest Frelinger, Ph.D., of the Yale
Department of Mental Hygiene. The gist of his findings is:
Psychoanalytically oriented psychologists are now "in a
discouraging position clearly not in the mainstream of
American psychology." Freud's influence is neither profound nor flourishing; papers on Behavior Modification
dominated at the previous annual session of the American
Psychology Association: there is no valid "outcome data"
substantiating the working of Freud's theories; Eysenck's
"biased outcome studies," exploding the therapeutic
claims of psychoanalysis, was a severe blow to the movement; Freud's theories are as rigid and unworkable as ever
after seventy years, whereas new developments in chemistry and physics occur every day; a "sense of stagnation"
oppressed him. Frelinger also asserted that medical
psychoanalysts are equally pessimistic and discouraged
over the complexities of Freud's theories.

In conclusion, Frelinger suggests collecting further observations toward a more "comprehensive view of man."
Clearly this advocates abandoning Freud and realizing
that he misled, bamboozled and tricked them as ruthlessly
as his patients. The fickle public now resists the lure of the
couch, by all current indications.

The decline can be attributed to greed. As Freud's
propaganda lured more and more to the couch, higher and
higher fees and longer courses were demanded. A corresponding inflation was effected in training analyses. With
greater power, more and more candidates were rejected,
for fear they would not remain true believers. The rejected,

numbering about one-fourth of the candidates, now constitute a considerable number and their hostility is effective.

It is interesting to compare these very recent professional publications revealing the current status of
psychoanalysis with material in a very popular lay
magazine, published in 1960. "Psychiatry, The Troubled
Science,"[12] contains this remarkable statement on the
combination of research and therapy in psychoanalysis:

"Dr. Karl Menninger points out that although
psychoanalysis does benefit patients, it would be
doomed if this were its main goal. The knowledge
gained from using psychoanalysis as a research tool,
he says, will help psychiatrists find quicker and less
expensive ways to treat patients."

The material from the professional journals which has
been cited, complete contradicts Menninger's assertion. In
fact, the exorbitant costs of psychoanalysis could be the
consequences of combining research and therapy, two conflicting, incompatible aims. In research, observation without interfering with the disorder is the prime consideration; in therapy, the patient's welfare demands correcting
a disorder.

According to the *Look* article, psychoanalysts contend
that high fees are "part of the treatment and not merely
payment for treatment. . . . a patient must pay a fee high
enough to constitute a sacrifice. Nor should he pay out of
his salary; more properly the money should come out of his
savings because analysis is a capital investment in himself."

Obviously then, the first requisite for psychoanalysis is
the ability to pay. Haak, a Swedish analyst who has "written extensively on the importance of high fees," is the
authority quoted for these arrogant demands. He contends
that an analyst charging high fees imparts a frank, forth-
right image to his patient, a fine person then to emulate.
High fees prevent feeling infantile and dependent upon
the analyst; neurotic patients who like to hurt themselves
find paying high fees an "excellent outlet for neurotic
feelings." On the other hand, low fees would "cause the

analyst to doubt his own motives; he might wonder if he was in love with the patient or if the really hates him and is trying to cover up by being kind. It is only fair that the analyst be adequately compensated for all the sufferings the patient heaps upon him."

The last statement lets the cat out, and intimates that analysts practice a futile, boring and tedious profession which also exposes them to the abuse of difficult and demanding patients. Therefore they console themselves with charging high fees despite dismal results.

The results of treatment — paying high fees — justifies such suspicion. A girl entering analysis at twenty-eight was forbidden to marry as it violated the "no decision" rule during analysis. At forty-two she was still on the couch and still unmarried. However, according to the analysts consulted in preparing the article, patients are strengthened by analysis. One is quoted:

"Where else can a patient lie down and be invited to talk about anything that pops into his mind? He can talk about himself, his wife, his boss, of the past, present or future; he need not be fair, considerate or objective, knowing that his unseen listener will neither scold nor disapprove."

The gruesome course of treatment, as described by the analysts, leaves the unmistakeable impression that it is the analyst who heaps the suffering upon the patient and not the patient upon the analyst as Haak complained. At first, the patient talks freely, but soon starts wondering when the problem solving will start. When the doctor fails "to utter the magic, curative words," he becomes more childlike and dependent, and "regresses to infancy." Regression is followed by frustration and anger at the lack of help. This stage may last for months, with suffering greater than before treatment.

The analysts quoted justified allowing this suffering because "in order to feel better the patient must first feel worse." Neurotic illness, they say, is caused by obscure memories, neither fully remembered nor forgotten. (This of course harks back to Freud's days with Breuer and makes nonsense of all their pretensions in justifying high fees, rambling incoherent discourses, continued suffering, etc., etc. If obscure memories should be revived, recall can be quickly effected, as Freud so easily did before inventing psychoanalysis).

Instead, the patient is allowed to regress until he thinks the analyst cruelly refused to help and blames him for his frustration. It is desirable to allow him to express his rage, they aver. This must be the "abuse heaped upon them," which justifies the high fees.

The treatment continues, so they say, until the crucial stage of transference arrives and the patient sees his analyst (tormentor) "not as he is, but through the colored bias of childhood. According to how he sees him, he will shower the analyst with hatred or love."

According to the theory, the analyst then will dissolve the transference and the patient is relieved. According to Freud, however, the transference persists even though the patient may never see his analyst again. As has been mentioned, the transference is really a state of hypnotism in which delusions as well as beneficial suggestions are equally easy to induce. When an analyst, purportedly a physician collecting fees for his services, is heaped with "hatred or love" instead of being regarded in a purely professional light, it is a dangerous state of delusion.

Among all the branches of medicine, psychiatry is unique in this respect: Psychiatrist and patient must talk a common language and communicate on intimate terms. Other physicians do not have to explain how a drug or treatment works, although they may. Surgeons are entirely out of communication with their patients on the operating table.

Because of the necessity of constant communication with the public, new developments in psychology are constantly publicized. The increasing cognizance of the decline in psychoanalysis prompted a newspaper feature, "Freud's Couch Giving Way to 'Now' Therapy."[13] In it, Dr. Judd Marmor contrasted the treatment of claustrophobia fifteen or twenty years ago with today's. Then, four or five

times a week for three to five years at a cost of $30,000 or
so, would be devoted to tracing the history of her entire life.
Today, she would be treated once or twice a week for six
months or even less, Dr. Marmor stated, using several
approaches which constitute a revolutionary departure
from the classical Freudian technique.

Several analysts rebuttals were published[14] under the
headline "Freud Analysis Theory Is Still Basic Doctrine in
Psychiatry." The first rebuttal denied that newer, shorter
methods were successful without offering any disproof nor
proof that psychoanalysis usually succeeds. The writer
then repeated the old propaganda that Freud's theories
have "been modified continually, is the basic science of
modern clinical psychiatry and virtually every
psychotherapist uses it constantly whether or not he acknowledges it."

The Frelinger article completely contradicted this claim
and called for a more comprehensive study of behavior
*sans* Freud.

"What is most difficult for all people to deal with,"
continued the same letter writer, "is the unvarnished
truth about ourselves. That is why psychoanalysis
will never become really popular and why we search
for methods of treatment that will not rely upon it.
Unfortunately we have not found it yet, as your article implied."

But the article plainly implied the new methods were
successful because they departed from Freud's long, un-
successful methods. The "unvarnished truth about ourselves," is of course the Oedipus complex, which we hypo-
critically deny only to incur neurotic suffering, according
to the Freudians.

A second correspondent dismissed the new approaches
as "scientific sounding terms and fads," useless to the
increasing numbers seeking psychiatric help. Then he
contradicted himself by admitting "some of these new
forms have their place in the psychiatric armamentarium
and many of the therapists who practice them have their
roots in psychoanalysis, but they are not the cure-all or the

new revolution." Obliquely, this acknowledges the new approaches are effective ("have a place") and they have been adopted by former Freudians ("therapists with their roots in psychoanalysis.")

The third correspondent, completely orthodox and dedicated, averred:

"To imply that the 'punch' is being taken out of psychoanalysis is to deprive many patients from the only treatment modality available for their particular type of disturbance."

Since Freud himself could not distinguish between mild and serious cases, that is neuroses from psychoses and Franz Alexander admitted as much himself, this argument appears specious. In addition, since the validity of the libido theory is now contested, as well as that sexual difficulties do not necessarily imply a neurosis, nor sexual potency guarantee its absence, then the diagnostic accuracy of psychoanalysis can no longer be trusted.

And this dogma, so impossible to apply with demonstrable benefit, was the creation of a man who detested being a physician, a man who was possessed and burdened by abnormal predilections, with a pathological itch both for intimacy and riches and fame. To promote his egomanic inclinations, he used his considerable energy, literary talent and awesome hypnotic powers to create a profession in which the indolent, the indifferent and the incompetent not only survived but for a time succeeded in dominating psychology.

# References

### CHAPTER 1
1. "Problems in Technique . . ." *Psychoanalytic Review*, 1930, 17,
2. Freud, S. *Basic Writings*, N.Y., Modern Library, 1938
3. *biography of an idea*, N.Y., Simon & Schuster, 1965
4. Freud, S. "Autobiography," *Basic Writings*
5. Gindes, B.C. *New Concepts of Hypnosis*, N.Y., Julian Pr., 1951
6. Freud, S. *New Introductory Lectures*, N.Y., Norton 1933


### CHAPTER 2
1. Letter to Arnold Zweig, June 22, 1936
2. Freud, S. *Moses and Monotheism*, N.Y., Knopf, 1939
3. Wittels, Fritz *Sigmund Freud*, London, Allen & Unwin, 1924
4. Freud, S. *Letters to Fliess*, N.Y., Basic Books, 1954
5. Stone, Irving *Passions of the Mind*, N.Y., Doubleday 1971
6. Bennett, Ed. A., *C. G. Jung*, London, Barrie 1961
7. Jung, C.G., *Memories, Dreams, Reflections*, N.Y., Pantheon 1961
8. Bernfeld, S. "Freud's Scientific Beginnings," *American Imago*, 1949
9, 10. Jung, *Memories, Dreams, Reflections*
11. Bennett, *C. G. Jung,*
12. Sachs, Hans *Freud, Master & Friend*, Harvard, 1964
13, 14. Jung, *Memories, Dreams, Reflections*


### CHAPTER 3
1, 2. Jones, Ernest *Life & Work of Sigmund Freud*, N.Y., Basic Bk, 1953
3. "An Unknown Biographical Fragment," *Amer. Imago*, 1946, V4
4. N.Y., Knopf, 1939
5. "An Unknown Biographical Fragment,"
6. Freud, S., *An Outline of Psychoanalysis*, N.Y., Norton 1939
7. "Three Contributions to . . . Sexuality," *Basic Writings*
8. "The Interpretations of Dreams," *Ibid.*
9. N.Y., Doubleday, 1971

## CHAPTER 4

1, 2, 3. Jones, E. *Life of Sigmund Freud,*
4. Vienna, Deuticke, 1895
5. Freud, S., "An Autobiography," *Basic Writings*
6. *Collected Papers,* 5 Vols, London, Hogarth, 1938
7. *In Eigener Sache,* Berlin, 1906
8. *Letters . . . to Fliess,* N.Y. Basic, 1964


## CHAPTER 5

1. Freud, S. "Interpretation of Dreams," *Basic Writings*
2. "A General Introduction to Psychoanalysis," *Ibid.,*
3, 4. Sachs, *Freud, Master and Friend,*
5, 6. "Psychopathology of Every-Day Life," *Basic Writings*
7. *Collected Papers,* 5 vols, London, Hogarth, 1938
8. Jones, E. *Life of Sigmund Freud,*


## CHAPTER 6

1, 2. N.Y., Grune & Stratton, 1963


## CHAPTER 7

1. *Psychoanalytic Quarterly,* 1940
2. Alexander, F., *Medical Value of Psychoanalysis,* N.Y., Norton, 1932
3. Alexander, F., French, F. *Psychoanalytic Therapy,* N.Y., Roland, 1946
4. *Collected Papers,*
5. *Atlantic Monthly,* July, 1964
6. N.Y., Doubleday, 1957


## CHAPTER 8

1. N.Y., Simon & Schuster, 1954
2. N.Y., Hellman, Williams, 1947
3. Evans, R.I., "Gordon Allport — A Conversation," *Psychology Today,* April 1971
4. London, Hogarth, 1959
5. Bernays, Edward, *biography of an idea,* N.Y., S&S, 1965
6. Rosenbaum, M., "Psychoanalysis at the Hebrew University," *Journal of American Psychoanalytic Ass'n,* April, 1954
7. Harms, E. "Jung, Defender of Freud and the Jews" *Psychiatric Quarterly,* 1946, Vol. 20, p199
8. Springfield, Charles Thomas, 1965
9. Masserman, J., ed *Science & Psychoanalysis,* N.Y. Grune & Stratton, 1966
10. Cambridge, Houghton Mifflin, 1966
11. *Science News,* January 28, 1967

## CHAPTER 10

1. Jung, *Memories, Dreams, Reflections,*
2. Freeman, Erika "Theodore Reik — A Conversation" *Psych. Today* April 1972
3. Roazen, P. *Brother Animal,* N.Y., Knopf, 1969
4. Weiss, E. *Agoraphobia in the Light of Ego Psychology,* N.Y., Grune & Stratton, 1964
5. Whyte, Lancelot L. *Unconscious Before Freud* N.Y., Basic Bks, 1960


## CHAPTER 11

1. *International Journal of Psychoanalysis,* Part 1, 1973
2. *Journal of American Psychoanalytic Ass'n,* June 1970
3. Blanton, S. *Diary of My Analysis with Freud,* N.Y., Hawthorn, 1971
4. "History of the Psychoanalytic Movement," *Basic Writings*
5. *Bulletin of the Menninger Clinic,* XXXVI, 1, 2, 1972
6. *Journal American Academy of Psychoanalysis,* 1973, 193-207
7. N.Y., Norton 1958
8. "To Be a God," *Commentary,* 1963, 36, 125-135
9. French, T. M. *Integration of Behavior,* U of Chicago Press, 1952
10. *Journal of American Psychoanalytic Ass'n,* April 1970
11. *Psychoanalytic Quarterly,* No. 1, 1972
12. Berg, Roland H. *Look* Feb. 2, 1960
13. Shaw, David *Los Angeles Times,* Feb. 13, 1972.
14. *Los Angeles Times,* Feb. 24, 1972

# Date Due